The STAMP COLLECTOR'S HANDBOOK

A VALUABLE STOREHOUSE OF PHILATELIC KNOWLEDGE

FOR PLEASURE OR FOR INVESTMENT

by

SAMUEL GROSSMAN

GROSSMAN STAMP CO., Inc.

860 BROADWAY, NEW YORK, N. Y. 10003

First printing April 1957
Second printing January 1958
Third printing April 1959
Fourth printing April 1960
Fifth printing January 1961
Sixth printing January 1962
Seventh printing March 1963
Eighth printing December 1964
Ninth printing April 1966
Tenth printing April 1968
Eleventh printing June 1970
Twelfth printing January 1972
Thirteenth printing February 1973
Fourteenth printing October 1973
Fifteenth printing January 1975

Library of Congress Catalog Card Number 57-9037

PRINTED IN THE U.S.A.

THIS BOOK IS DEDICATED

TO THE MEMORY OF MY

BELOVED SON, MARTIN.

1939 - 1946

FOREWORD

In presenting the factors underlying the collecting of postage stamps, I have assumed the reader has not the least knowledge of the hobby. With this in mind, it has been my effort to imbue the fundamentals with simplicity as much as possible. My paramount object is to enable any child or adult without the faintest knowledge of stamps to be able to grasp these most interesting chapters.

Supplementing the principles are other matter of related or informative interest including tables, guides, a glossary of philatelic terms and an encyclopedic dictionary-index.

For rendering welcome assistance on some of the illustrative and text material the author wishes to express thankful acknowledgment to the Bureau of Engraving and Printing, Washington, D.C. and the Philatelic Department of the Post Office. Also may be added Hammermill Paper Co. and the American Paper Institute. For also contributing towards this undertaking I likewise am indebted for the valued and gracious co-operation of such famed and distinguished authorities as R.E. Fellers, former Director of Philately, Post Office Department, Bernard D. Harmer. Robert A. Siegel and Raymond H. Weill.

Since the first printing of this work, I have received many kind and complimentary letters for which I take this opportunity to acknowledge with deepest gratitude. However amidst these were occasionally found well intentioned comments of a controversial or correctory nature. These always receive not only due respect and consideration on my part but also my sincere thanks. With the fullest appreciation, I always welcome any co-operative endeavor to bring this handbook to the highest state of perfection.

It is most rewarding to know that this edition not only represents the Fifteenth Printing of this handbook but still maintains its reputation as ever of being the fastest selling Philatelic Publication of its type.

S.G.

CONTENTS

YOU ENTER A FABULOUS NEW WORLD

The strains imposed by competitive strife, the woes of an uneasy world or perhaps the montony of an uneventful daily routine are exactions on the human faculties from which the human machine requires restful diversion and mental refreshment.

This can be furnished by a rejuvenating and absorbing pastime like stamp collecting, which is recommended by leading educators throughout the world. The collecting of stamps offers refuge to the confused and gives new vigor to fallen spirits. It shuts the door to problems and perplexities. And this is not all. In the midst of the many delightful moments spent on this fascinating hobby of kings, it is with little effort that you become familiar with the culture of many lands, their arts, their traditions and folklore. You will also find yourself delving into history, zoology, botany, geography, politics, mythology, painting, sculpture, world progress, architecture and biography. It represents a full-fledged course for self-education.

Collecting stamps requires industry, concentration, research and intelligence. For that reason a youngster's association with other stamp collectors will bring him into contact with wholesome company, which is of incalculable importance in shaping his future character and inclinations. Stamp collecting is encouraged by the Boy and Girl Scouts of America and other National Youth Organizations.

While this hobby is very popular with royalty and the rich it need not be confined to the upper crust. A large stamp collection may be built up with a small outlay, as there are many thousands of stamps within reach of the purse of the most thrifty buyer. There can be just as much enjoyment out of the cheaper grade of stamps as from the scarcest specimens. It must be brought out that true appreciation of stamps is in their study and not merely in their accumulation or value. Number and even rarity are of only secondary importance.

Those entering the gates of Philately (Stamp Collecting) have awaiting them an uncountable number of new-found joys, interests, and entertaining moments. It offers adventure, contact with the mysticism of the East, reveals the rise and fall of nations, and thousands of new-found thrills. You will live many lives as you become intrigued by these unending delights.

It is with these happy prospects that there will be unfolded to the reader through the suceeding chapters this fabulous new world.

Roman Post Chariot. Cuneiform Writing. Ancient Indian Messenger 2500 B.C.

EARLY POST SYSTEMS BEFORE THE ADHESIVE STAMP

The first official postage stamp was issued by Great Britain in 1840. This did not represent a discovery of the postal system. It was rather a major improvement over the prior era of stampless covers (folded letters).

Postal systems go back thousands of years, even perhaps to about 3,500 B.C. when the Sumerians of ancient Mesopotamia developed the cuneiform system of writing impressed on stone, clay brick and tablets. Such messages have been unearthed by excavations of their ruins and that of their successors, the Babylonians, Assyrians and Persians. The phrase "Neither snow nor rain, nor heat nor gloom of night stays these couriers from the swift completion of their appointed rounds," which adorns the facade of the general post office in New York City, was coined in 485 B.C. by Herodotus the Greek traveler and historian, in his admiration of the post systems of the Persians.

The early Greek and Roman post systems were carried out in relays by the fleet of foot and by horse. Pigeon posts and carriages were also used in those days. Post systems are known to have been established by the pharaohs of ancient Egypt, Charlemagne, the holy Roman Emperors, King Henry VIII of Great Britain, and the leaders of the Hanseatic League of Towns, etc. The Incas and Aztecs of the Western Hemisphere used runners for their highly efficient post systems. See Scott's No. 360 of Peru. Hardly any power in the past did not have some form of post system. This was a necessity to maintain authority, collect taxes and tribute, as well as to be alerted in case of insurrection or impending invasion.

Inca Courier. Mercury, Messenger of the Gods. Message by arrow.

A stampless cover of the pre-postage stamp era.

As Genghis Khan (1162-1227), the great Mongol Conquerer, extended his empire over vast areas of plains, deserts and mountains, he established along his route well organized and efficient posts. Between these went dispatches of army communications and matters of state. His grandson, Kublai Khan, further improved this system, establishing over 10,000 postal and refreshment stations, with riders traveling back and forth day and night with frequent changes of horses. The Venetian traveler Marco Polo mentioned that messages of urgency were forwarded at the rate of 250 miles per day.

At first serving only the royal princes in Europe since the 15th century, the House of Thurn and Taxis opened up its postal system to the public in 1505. It continued to operate throughout Europe until 1867-72, during which times its use by certain German States was superseded by those of the unified German Empire.

With improvements in speed due to developments in steam and electric locomotion, motor vehicles, airplanes, etc., the postal system attained its present high degree of speed and efficiency.

For centuries the old posts served only royalty, the nobility, and the church. They were also used for war communications, matters of state, and urgency. In time this service was extended to business houses, important merchants, and favorites of the court and universities. It was not available to the average citizen. Anyhow, few people in those times knew how to read or

Portrait of Francis of Taxis and two stamps of the Thurn and Taxis postal system.

Sir Rowland Hill and the first two postage stamps; (1840) 1p black and 2p blue.

write. By progressive stages, messages were first written on stone and clay tablets, then on papyrus, wax, and parchment, and eventually on paper as in modern times.

In 1680, an efficient penny post system was established by William Dockwra in London with over 400 receiving stations. He is supposed to have been the first to have originated the postmark indicating the date, time, and place of mailing. Dockwra conflicted with James, Duke of York, and his post office was taken over and incorporated into the government postal service.

At the time adhesive stamps were first used in 1840, the sender usually folded the letter paper so that it formed both the message and wrapper together. There was usually a wax seal on the back. If an envelope was used it was usually hand-made. These so-called stampless covers were sent collect with rates determined by the distance and weight. When letters were refused, the government had no means of exacting payment.

It was Sir Rowland Hill, father of the modern postal system, who originated low postal rates and instituted advanced ideas and reforms in the postal system of Great Britain during the reign of Queen Victoria. He reduced the distance rate on ordinary letters from one ·shilling to one penny, payable in advance. This rate of postage was determined by weight and not by distance. In 1840, Rowland Hill introduced in Great Britain the first adhesive postage stamps. This was the one penny black, which came out simultaneously with the next denomination, the two penny blue. Both were imperforated, and the stamps had to be cut apart by scissors or other means. Hill also commissioned William Mulready of the Royal Academy of Art to design a stamped envelope. This Mulready envelope and the first two adhesive stamps went into use in England on May 6, 1840. The two stamps met with tremendous success. The public bought them not only for postal use but also out of admiration, and for their value as souvenirs. However, the Mulready envelope, although of elaborate and artistic design, was received with ridicule. Caricatures appeared in the press and leading periodicals. The result was that most

Mulready Envelope (1840)

of these Mulready covers were withdrawn and destroyed by
the post office. Both the original covers and caricatures are
now highly prized by collectors.

In the United States about 1842, Alexander Greig operated
a private City Despatch Post in New York City, where he set
up mail boxes. He issued stamps, but those who bought 100
or more were given a discount. This post was purchased in
August 1842, by the New York Post Office and continued as
the United States City Despatch Post. Its 3c stamp of that year
is the first adhesive stamp issued in the western hemisphere.
With the consent of the Federal Postmasters, other cities fol-
lowed with similar issues. Among them were St. Louis, Mo.,
New Haven, Conn., Brattleboro, Vt., Providence, R. I., and
Baltimore, Md. In 1847, the Federal Government issued its
first regular stamps, the 5c red brown and 10c black, and all
Postmaster Provisional Issues were discontiued.

1842 Greig's 3c City Despatch Post; Postmaster Provisional Issues:
5c Providence, R. I. (1846); 5c Millbury, Mass. (1846).

The first two regular U.S. postage stamps. 5c red brown and 10c black (1847).

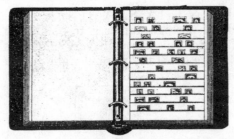 

STAMP COLLECTORS' EQUIPMENT

The following accessories may in part of or whole comprise the equipment of a serious stamp collector's laboratory. Outside of the elementary requirements such as stamp album, hinges and mounts there should be included a perforation gauge, stamp tongs, watermark detector, watermark fluid, magnifying glass, stock book, Scott's Standard Catalog and any other helpful reference books. The perforation gauge and watermark detector will be discussed in further chapters.

Stamp Tongs (or Tweezers)

A very essential instrument for the proper handling of stamps. Enables stamps to be handled without coming into contact with unclean or greasy fingers. With experience specimens of stamps can with tweezers be picked up with speed and dexterity. Usually furnished in either spade, round or pointed ends, depending upon the taste of the customer. The spade ends are usually the most popular. Be sure that the ends of pointed tweezers are not too pointed so that they may possibly damage the stamps. In selecting tweezers, also note whether the two prongs meet evenly and whether they are of a tension suitable to the pressure from your fingers.

Magnifying Glass

A good magnifying glass is very necessary in the study of stamps. Definitely required to identify the various printing processes, also to note the various types, secret marks and finer points of stamps. A good philatelic magnifier should be strong, sharp and clear right to the very rim of the instrument. These may come in various styles, as reader, folded or on stands.

Stock Book

The sheets of this book have rows of cardboard or transparent (acetate) pockets into which stamps can be more or less firmly held. This enables the owner to store stamps for most any purpose without the use of adhesives. Sheets of stock books are usually interchangeable which will aid system and expansion.

HOW TO IDENTIFY STAMPS

The first step in the study of postage stamps is to be able to determine the country of origin. This is usually very simple, as the names of the countries are generally printed right on the stamps.

As an example, on the above stamps the names of the countries, Ceylon and Hong Kong are plainly inscribed on the stamps. It is just as simple with most other stamps. Sometimes the foreign names of the countries may be a little different than the accustomed English names, but there will be enough similarity to leave no doubt as to the identity. As an example, on stamps below, it can easily be ascertained that Nederland means Netherlands, and that Danmark means Denmark.

Therefore, only a little common sense is required in making out the names of most countries. There are some cases where the beginner may have some difficulty in identifying stamps. However there are usually other clues when the foreign names are difficult to ascertain. One may be able to determine the country of origin of a foreign stamp by examining name, inscriptions, scenes, currency, portraits, overprints, etc.

The stamp to the left above, contains a map of Ireland and is obviously an Irish stamp. The stamp to the right above has the inscription MAGYAR POSTA. Although there is no phonetic similarity between the names of MAGYAR and HUNGARY, it is, however, common knowledge to most people that these names indicate the same country.

NOTE: As a further help, you may refer to "AID IN IDENTIFYING STAMPS," and "ILLUSTRATED STAMP IDENTIFIER" which follows.

GUIDE TO IDENTIFYING STAMPS

Some countries are known by two or more names. As an example the names of Ireland, Eire and Irish Free State all refer to the same country. However that particular name adopted by Scott's Standard Catalog is accepted as the principal name and as such will be revealed in all capital letters through checking names in question against the list below. For identification purposes, this procedure also applies to unusual and unintellegible foreign names. Where no name appears on a stamp there may be other wordage thereon which may lead to its identity such as inscriptions, overprints, currency, abbreviations, etc. Likewise these could be matched below for revealing the possible origin of a stamp. Where a stamp is completely destitute of any wordings whatsoever, the Illustrated Stamp Identifier which follows may be resorted to.

Ab. Currency of BULGARIA.
Abyssinia. Also known as ETHIOPIA.
Acores. Native name for AZORES.
Aegean Is. In Scott's under ITALY.
Aent, Aenton. EPIRUS.
Afghan, Afghanes. AFGHANISTAN.
Afrique Equatoriale Africa. FRENCH EQUATORIAL AFRICA.
Afrique Occidentale Franc. FRENCH WEST AFRICA.
Africa Orientale Italiana. ITALIAN EAST AFRICA.
Alexandria. FRANCE. Offices in Egypt.
Allemagne Duitschland. French for GERMANY.
Alsace. Listed under FRANCE.
Alwar. A state in north INDIA.
Anatolia. TURKEY IN ASIA.
Anna. Currency usually of INDIA.
Antioquia. A dept. of COLOMBIA.
A Payer. BELGIUM and Col's Postage Due.
Apaxmai. Inscription on stamps of GREECE.
Avisporto. Newspaper stamps of DENMARK.
Bahawalpur. A state of PAKISTAN.
Bai. Currency of ROMAGNA.
Baj. Currency of ROMAN STATES.
Bamra. A state of INDIA.
Bani. Currency of ROMANIA.
Baranya. Overprints. Indicates Serbian Occ.
Barwani. A state of INDIA.
Basel. A canton of SWITZERLAND.
Bayern. The native name for BAVARIA.
Belgian Congo. CONGO.
Belgie, Belgique. BELGIUM.
Benadir. ITALIAN SOMALILAND.
Berlin. Occupation Overprints. GERMANY.
Bhopal. A state in INDIA.
Bohemia and Moravia. In CZECHOSLOVAKIA.

Bohmen and Mahren. Same as above.
Bolivar. A dept. of COLOMBIA REP.
Borneo. NORTH BORNEO.
Boyaca. A dept. of COLOMBIA REP.
Brasil. The native name for BRAZIL.
Braunschweig. BRUNSWICK.
British New Guinea. PAPUA.
British Somaliland. SOMALILAND PROTECTORATE.
British South Africa. RHODESIA.
Buenos Aires. A prov. and city of ARGENTINA.
Bussahir. A state in INDIA.
CCCP. Inscription on stamps of RUSSIA.
C.G.H.S. Overprints. UPPER SILESIA.
Cabo-Juby Native name for CAPE JUBY
Calchi. Under ITALY—Aegean Islands Overprint.
Calino. Under ITALY—Aegean Islands Overprint.
Canton. Under FRANCE—Offices in China.
Cárinthia. Under AUSTRIA and JUGOSLAVIA.
Capatho-Ukraine Under CZECHOSLOVAKIA.
Caso. Under ITALY—Aegean Islands Overprint.
Cauca. A dept. of COLOMBIA REP.
Cavalle. Under FRANCE—Offices in Turkey.
Cesko Slovensko. Native name. CZECHOSLOVAKIA.
Chamba. A state in INDIA.
Charkhari. A state in INDIA.
Chiffre Taxe. Indicates due stamps of FRANCE.
Chosen. The Jap name for KOREA.
Cirenaica. CYRENAICA.
Cochin. A state in INDIA.
Colonia de Rio de Oro. RIO DE ORO.
Comoro Islands. GRAND COMORO ISLANDS.

Comunicaciones. SPAIN. Implies postal serv.

Constantinopli. Overprint. ITALY—Off. Turkey.

Coo. Under ITALY. Aegean Islands. Overprint.

Cordoba (Cordova). A province in ARGENTINA.

Corea. KOREA.

Corrientes. A province in ARGENTINA.

Cos. Under ITALY—Aegean Islands. Overprint.

Cote D'Somalia. French for SOMALI COAST.

Cpbnja. Inscription on stamps of SERBIA.

Ctotankh. Inscription on stamps of BULGARIA.

Cundinamarca. A dept. of COLOMBIA REP.

Danmark. Native name for DENMARK.

Dansk Vestindian. DANISH WEST INDIES.

Dedeagh. Under FRANCE. Offices in Turkey.

De L'Oceanie. French for FRENCH OCEANIA.

Del Golfo de Guinea. SPANISH GUINEA.

Deutsche Bundespost. GERMANY. Federal Rep.

Deutsche Demokratische. GERMANY. East.

Deutsche Neu Guinea. GERMAN NEW GUINEA.

Deutsche Ostafrika. GERMAN EAST AFRICA.

Deutsche Sudwestafrika. GERMAN SOUTH-WEST AFRICA.

Deutsches Reich. Native name for GERMANY.

Dhar. A state in INDIA.

Dienstmarke. GERMANY or DANZIG. Official stamps.

Djibouti. A port. Under SOMALI COAST.

Doplata. Ins. on stamps of POLAND and CENTRAL LITHUANIA.

Drzavna. Inscription on stamps of JUGOSLAVIA.

Duitsch Oost Afrika. GERMAN EAST AFRICA.

Durazzo. Overprint. ITALY—Off. in Turkey.

Dutch Guiana. Under SURINAM.

East Africa. BRITISH EAST AFRICA.

Eesti. Native name. ESTONIA.

Egeo. Overprints or Ins. ITALY—Aegean Islands.

Einzuziehen. Indicates postage dues. DANZIG.

Eire. Native name. IRELAND.

Eireann. Overprints. Under IRELAND.

Empire Franc. French for French Empire. FRANCE.

Enapiomon. Inscription on stamps of GREECE.

England. Under GREAT BRITAIN.

En. Currency of JAPAN.

Eonikh. Inscription on stamps of GREECE.

Establissements Francais Dans L'Indie French for FRENCH INDIA.

Escuelas. Ins. on stamps of VENEZUELA.

Espana, Espanola. Native names for SPAIN.

Espresso. Indicates special delivery. ITALY.

Estado da India. PORTUGUESE INDIA.

Estero. Overprint. ITALY—Offices in China.

Eupen and Malmedy. GERMANY. Belgian Occupation.

Faridkot. A state in INDIA.

Federated Malay States. Under STRAITS SETTLEMENTS.

Feldpost, K.u.K. AUSTRIA. Military Mail.

Fen, Fn. Currency of MANCHUKUO.

Fezzen. LIBIA. French Occupation. stamps.

Filipinas. Native name for PHILIPPINES.

Franco Bollo Postale. Inscription on stamps of ITALY, ROMAN STATES, SARDINIA, etc.

Frei durch Ablosung. GERMANY. Local Off'ls.

General Gouvernement. Under POLAND.

Ghadames. Under LIBIA, Fezzan-Ghadames.

Ghana. Native name for GOLD COAST.

Gd. Liban. Native name for LEBANON.

Graham Land. Overprint. FALKLAND IS.

Grand Liban. LEBANON.

Gronland. Danish name for GREENLAND.

Guanacaste. A prov. of COSTA RICA.

Guinea Espanole. SPANISH GUINEA.

Guinee. FRENCH GUINEA.

Guyane Francaise. FRENCH GUIANA.

Gwalior. A state in INDIA.

Hashemite Kingdom. Under TRANS-JORDAN.

Haute Silesie. French for UPPER SILESIA.

Haute Volta. French for UPPER VOLTA.

Hellas. Native name for GREECE.

Heller. Currency on former stamps of AUSTRIA, LIECHTENSTEIN, BOSNIA, etc.

Helvetia. Native name for SWITZERLAND.

HOby. As currency. MONTENEGRO.

Hoi Hao. Operprint. FRANCE—Off. China.

Holkar. State in INDIA.

Holland. Under NETHERLANDS.

Hrvatska. Native name for CROATIA.

Hyderabad. A state in INDIA.

Iiapa. Ins. on SERBIA· and MONTENEGRO.

Iioptomapka. Ins. on stamps of MONTENEGRO.

Iipha. Inscriptions on stamps of MONTENEGRO.

Ile Rouad. Overprints. Under ROUAD.

Iles Wallis et Futuna. WALLIS & FUTUNA IS.

Imperio Colonial Portuguese. PORTUGUESE COL'S.

Impto de Guerra. SPAIN. War tax stamps.

Indore or Holkar. State in INDIA.

Ingermanland. NORTH INGERMANLAND.

Inkeri. Ins. on NORTH INGERMANLAND.

Inner Mongolia. Under CHINA.

Instruccion. VENEZUELA. School tax stamps.

IDENTIFYING STAMPS

Iran. Native name for PERSIA.
Island. Native name for ICELAND.
Isole Italiane dell'Egeo. ITALY—Aegean Islands.
Isole Jonie. Native name for IONIAN IS.
Istria. Under JUGOSLAVIA.
Italia, Italiane. Native names for ITALY.
Jaipur. A state in INDIA.
Jammu and Kashmir. A state in INDIA.
Janina. Overprints. ITALY—Off. in Turkey.
Java. Under DUTCH INDIES.
Jhalawar. A state in INDIA.
Jhind. A state in INDIA.
Johore. Under STRAITS SETTLEMENTS.
Jordan. Under TRANS-JORDAN.
K.u.K. Feldpost. Ins. on stamps of AUSTRIA.
K.u.K. Feldpost. Ins. with Bani or Lei currency. ROMANIA.
K.u.K. Militarpost. Ins. on Austrian stamps. BOSNIA AND HERZEGOVINA.
Kamerun. Former German colony of CAMEROONS.
Karki. Overprint. ITALY—Aegean Is.
Karolinen. CAROLINE IS. Former German Colony.
Kashmir. A state in INDIA.
Kathiri, State of. Under ADEN.
Kedah. Under STRAITS SETTLEMENTS.
Kelanton. Under STRAITS SETTLEMENTS.
Kishengarh. A state in INDIA.
Klaipeda. Native name for MEMEL.
Kon, Koh, Koli. Currency. Usually of RUSSIA.
Korca, Korce. Inscriptions on stamps of ALBANIA.
Kouang-Tcheou. Overprints. FRANCE—Off. in China.
Kraljevina. Inscription on stamps of JUGOSLAVIA.
Kraljevstvo. Ins. on stamps of JUGOSLAVIA.
Krone, Kronen. Currency AUSTRIA, DENMARK, NORWAY.
La Aguera. Native name for AGUERA.
La Canea. Under ITALY—Offices in Crete.
La Georgie. Native name for GEORGIA.
Laibach, Ljubljana, Lubiana. Under JUGOSLAVIA.
Lattaquie. Native name for Latakia.
Lero. Overprint. Under ITALY—Aegean Is.
Lei. Currency of ROMANIA.
Libanaise. Native name for LEBANON.
Libya. Under LIBIA.
Lietuwa. Native name for LITHUANIA.
L'Inini. French for ININI.
Lipso. Overprint. Under ITALY—Aegean Is.
Lisso. Overprint. Under ITALY—Aegean Is.
Litwa, Litwy. Native names of CENTRAL LITHUANIA.
L'Oceania. French for FRENCH OCEANIA.
Losen. Indicates due stamps of SWEDEN.
Lothraingen. Overprint. Under FRANCE. (Lorraine).
Magyar, Magyarorszag. Indicates HUNGARY.

Malacca. Under STRAITS SETTLEMENTS.
Malaya. Ins. on stamps of STRAITS SETTLEMENTS.
Malmedy. Under GERMANY. Belgian Occupation.
Mapka. Ins. on stamps of RUSSIA or FINLAND.
Maroc. French for FRENCH MOROCCO.
Marruecos. Under SPANISH MOROCCO.
Mejico. Native name for MEXICO.
Mocambique. Native name for MOZAMBIQUE.
Morocco Agencies. Under GREAT BRITAIN. Offices.
Morocco (French). Under FRENCH MOROCCO.
Morokko. Overprints. GERMANY, Off. in Morocco.
Moyen Congo. French for MIDDLE CONGO.
Morvi. State in INDIA.
Nabha. A state in INDIA.
Napa. Ins. on stamps of MONTENEGRO and SERBIA.
Nape. Inscriptions on stamps of SERBIA.
Ned. Indie. Under DUTCH INDIES.
Nederlandsch Indie. Under DUTCH INDIES.
Negri Sembilan. Under STRAITS SETTLEMENTS.
Nejd. Under SAUDI ARABIA.
Nezavisna. Inscription on stamps of CROATIA.
Nisiro. Overprint. Under ITALY—Aegean Islands.
Noptomapka. Inscription on stamps of MONTENEGRO.
Nopto Mapha. Inscription on stamps of SERBIA.
Norddeutsche Post. Ins. on early GERMANY.
Norge. Native name for NORWAY.
Nouvelle Calendonia. Under NEW CALEDONIA.
Nouvelle Hebrides. French for NEW HEBRIDES.
Nowanuggar. A state in INDIA.
Noyta. Ins. on stamps of RUSSIA and SOUTH RUSSIA.
Oceania (French). Under FRENCH OCEANIA.
Oil Rivers. Overprint. Under NIGER COAST.
Oranje Vrij Staat. Under ORANGE RIVER COLONY.
Orchha. A state in INDIA.
Ore. Currency used by DENMARK, NORWAY and SWEDEN.
Osterreich. Native name for AUSTRIA.
Ostland. Overprint. German Occ. of RUSSIA.
Ottomanes. Native name for TURKEY.
Oubangui-Chari-Tchad. Overprint. UBANGI.
Pacchi Postali. Indicates Parcel Post. Inscription on stamps of ITALY and SAN MARINO.
Pahang. Under STRAITS SETTLEMENTS.

Pakhoi. Overprints. Under FRANCE—Off. in China.

Patiala. A state in INDIA.

Patmo, Patmos. Under ITALY—Aegean Is. (Overprint).

PCCP. Inscription. Identifies RUSSIA.

Pechino. Overprint. Under ITALY—Off. in China.

Penang. Under STRAITS SETTLEMENTS.

Pen, Pennia. Currency used by FINLAND.

Perak. Under STRAITS SETTLEMENTS.

Perlis. Under STRAITS SETTLEMENTS.

Persane, Persanes. Native names for PERSIA.

Pies. Currency used by INDIA AND PAKISTAN.

Piscopi. Overprint. Under ITALY—Aegean Island.

Poczta Polska. Native name for POLAND.

Johjois. Native name for North Ingermanland.

Poonch. A state in INDIA.

Port Gdansk. Under POLAND—Off. in Danzig.

Port Cantonal. Identifies early SWITZERLAND.

Porteado. Ins. on PORTUGAL and PORTUGUESE COL'S.

Porto. With no country name, AUSTRIA.

Port Said. Under FRANCE. Offices in Egypt.

Portuguese East Africa. Under MOZAMBIQUE.

Portugcese Guinea. Under GUINEA.

Postas le nioc. Identifies dues of IRELAND.

Preussen. Native name for PRUSSIA.

Poste Locale. Identifies early SWITZERLAND.

Puerto Rico. PORTO RICO.

PYb, PYB. Usually inscriptions on RUSSIA.

Qu'aiti, State of. Under ADEN.

Qindar, Qinta. Currency of ALBANIA.

Rarotonga. Inscription on stamps of COOK IS.

Rayon. Ins. on Early SWITZERLAND.

Recargo. Identifies war tax stamps of SPAIN.

Reichpost. Refers to postal issues of GERMANY.

Reis. Currency used by PORTUGAL and BRAZIL. With no country name, usually PORTUGAL.

Repub. Franc. Refers to republic of FRANCE.

Rheinland-Pfalz. Under GERMANY. French Occ.

Rhodes. Under ITALY—Aegean Islands.

Rialar Sealdac Na Heireann. IRELAND Overprint.

RO. Overprint. Indicates EASTERN RUMELIA.

Rodi (or Rhodes). Under ITALY—Aegean Islands.

Roumania. ROMANIA.

Roumelie Orientale. Overprint. EASTERN RUMELIA.

Ruanda and Urundi. Under BELGIAN EAST AFRICA.

Rumania. ROMANIA.

S. Marino. Indicates SAN MARINO.

Saargebiet. Native name for SAAR.

Sachsen. Native name for SAXONY.

Sahara Espanol. SPANISH WESTERN SAHARA.

S. Tome E. Principe. ST. THOMAS AND PRINCE IS.

ST. CHRISTOPHER. Recent issued under ST. KITTS-NEVIS.

SE. MARIE DE MADAGASCAR. STE. of name same as St.

Sandjak D'Alexandretta. Under ALEXANDRETTA.

Santander. A state of COLOMBIA REP.

Saorstaat Eireann. Overprint. Indicates IRELAND.

Saurashtra. (or Soruth). A state of INDIA.

Scarpanto. Overprint. Under ITALY — Aegean Islands.

Scudo. Currency of ROMAN STATES.

Segna Tassa. (Segnatasse). Ins. on postage due stamps of ITALY, SAN MARINO and VATICAN CITY.

Selangor. Under STRAITS SETTLEMENTS.

Sen, Sn. Currency used in JAPAN.

Shqipni, Shqipare. Ins. on stamps of ALBANIA.

Simi. Overprint. Under ITALY—Aegean Is.

Singapore. Under STRAITS SETTLEMENTS.

Sirmoor (Sirmur). A state in INDIA.

Skilling. Currency used by DENMARK, NORWAY and SWEDEN.

Sld. Currency used by AUSTRIA—Off. in Turkey.

Sleswig. Under SCHLESWIG-HOLSTEIN.

Slovakia. A state of CZECHOSLOVAKIA.

Slovenia Carniola. Under JUGOSLAVIA.

Slovenska-Slovensko. Under JUGOSLAVIA.

Sn. Currency of JAPAN.

SO 1920. Overprints. EASTERN SILESIA.

Soldi. Currency of AUSTRIA—Lombardy Venetia.

Solomon Is. Under BRITISH SOLOMON ISLANDS.

Somalia. Under ITALIAN SOMALILAND.

Soruth (Saurashtra). A state in INDIA.

Soudan. FRENCH SUDAN.

Sourashtra (Soruth). A state in INDIA.

South Africa. UNION OF SOUTH AFRICA.

South Georgia. Overprint. FALKLAND IS.

South Orkneys. Overprint. FALKLAND IS.

South Shetlands. Overprint. FALKLAND ISLANDS.

Soviet Russia. Under RUSSIA.

Srodkowa. Indicates CENTRAL LITHUANIA.

Stampalia. Under ITALY—Aegean Is. (Overprint).

Suid-Afrika. Boer for UNION OF SOUTH AFRICA.

Suidwes. Boer for SOUTH-WEST AFRICA.

Sungei Ujong. Under STRAITS SETTLEMENTS.
YCCP. Overprint. UKRAINE.
Sverige. Native name for SWEDES.
S.W.A. Overprints SOUTH-WEST AFRICA.
Syrienne. Native name for SYRIA.
Takca. Indicates due stamps of BULGARIA.
Takse. Indicates stamp of ALBANIA.
Takcoha. Indicates MONTENEGRO.
Tanger. Under FRENCH MOROCCO or SPAN. MOROCCO.
Tangier. Overprints. Under GREAT BRITAIN. Offices in Morocco.
Tchad. CHAD.
Tchecoslovakia. CZECHOSLOVAKIA.
Tchongking. Overprint. FRANCE—Off. China.
Te Betalen. Ins. on due stamps of NETHERLANDS and COLONIES.
Thailand. SIAM.
Tjeneste. DENMARK. Inscription.
Tjenestefrimerke. NORWAY. Official mail.
Toga. TONGA.
Tolima. A dept. of COLOMBIA REP.

Tome E. Principe. ST. THOMAS AND PRINCE IS.
Touva TANNU TUVA.
Travencore. A state of INDIA.
Trengganu. Under STRAITS SETTLEMENTS.
Tripoli. Under LIBIA.
Ultramar. Usually CUBA or PORTO RICC.
Urundi. BELGIAN EAST AFRICA
Van Diemen's Land. Early name of TASMANIA.
Valona. Overprint. Under ITALY—Off. in Turkey.
Western Samoa. Under SAMOA.
YCCP. Overprint. UKRAINE.
Yen. Currency of JAPAN.
Ykpaichcbka. UKRAINE.
Yugoslavia JUGOSLAVIA.
Yunnan-Fou. Under FRANCE—Off. in China.
Z. Afr. Republiek. TRANSVAAL.
Zone Francaise. GERMANY. French Occupation.
Zuidwest Afrika. SOUTH-WEST AFRICA.
Zurich. SWITZERLAND.

1851 British Guiana cover with pair of two very rare 2¢ circular stamps for which was paid $71,400. Purchased by Weill.

INTAGLIO MULTICOLOR WEB PRESS (9-COLOR)

SEE HOW UNITED STATES STAMPS ARE PRINTED

See in work an ultra modern high speed nine color Intaglio press 100 feet long. The performance of this and other operations is included in the "Self Guided Free Tour" of the Bureau of Engraving and Printing, Washington, D. C. (See page 94)

ILLUSTRATED STAMP IDENTIFIER

This illustrated list applies to stamps which have no name thereon whatsoever or the foreign inscriptions or wordings are unintelligible in the English language. On such stamps the best means for identifications is through illustrations of which some of the most common examples follow below. In time with experience, the collector will readily recognize these himself, but in the start this list will prove convenient as well as instructive to the beginner. However do not resort to this list until you have first exhausted your efforts to identify a stamp through the STAMP IDENTIFIER

ABYSSINIA · AFGHANISTAN · ARMENIA · AUSTRIA · AZERBAIJAN · BATUM · BOSNIA & HERZEGOVINA · BRAZIL · BULGARIA · CHINA · COREA · DENMARK · EGYPT · FAR EASTERN REPUBLIC · GEORGIA · GREAT BRITAIN · GREECE · HEJAZ · HUNGARY · INDIA (Alwar) · INDIA (Bhopal) · INDIA (Faridkot) · INDIA (Hyderabad)

IDENTIFYING STAMPS

INDIA (Gwalior)

MONTENEGRO

STRAITS SETTLEMENTS

TURKEY
THESSALY

INDIA (Jhind)

THAILAND (Siam)

INDIA (Nowanuggur)

NEPAL

TURKEY IN ASIA

ISRAEL

PANAMA

THRACE

IRAN

PHILIPPINES

TRANSCAUCASIAN
Federated Republics

ROMAN STATES

TWO SICILIES

JAPAN

RUSSIA

TANNU TUVA

UKRAINIA

TURKEY

JORDAN   LATVIA

SAUDI ARABIA

LEBANON

SERBIA

MANCHUKUO

SOUTH RUSSIA

WESTERN UKRAINE

SPAIN

WHITE RUSSIA

19

Typical pages from an illustrated stamp album.

VARIOUS STAMP ALBUMS
HOW TO HINGE STAMPS-STAMP MOUNTS

After you have learned the identity of a stamp, your next move will be to place it in your album. Most collectors start out with an illustrated stamp album. These are generally arranged with the countries in alphabetical order, so it will not be difficult to find the country you desire. Also, you can refer to the index if the album has one. After you reach the country, then look for the design that resembles your stamp. This may be a single stamp or part of a series of similar or different stamps. You will therefore have to look for the specific space that corresponds with the denomination of your stamp. This also depends upon the type of album you have. If you have a rather small album, the spaces will be restricted to just the common or medium grade stamps. The more advanced the album is, the more complete it will be, and you will find more spaces for your stamps. Therefore it is always best to start out with as complete an album as you can afford.

If there is no space for a certain stamp, you may utilize whatever blank space is available nearby. If need be, you may also use spaces, whether blank or illustrated, to best suit your fancy or convenience. However, those having loose-leaf editions of illustrated stamp albums can solve the space problem by getting extra blank sheets. Otherwise, it is suggested that the collector provide himself with a supplementary stamp album.

Stamps should never be pasted down flat in the album. Do not use paste, glue or apply any adhesives for the purpose of attaching stamps. Nor should materials as mending tape, top of envelope, etc. be used for hinges. Good hinges are usually available from most stamp dealers. These should be thin and transparent and of the utmost importance, they should be peelable enough so that any can be removed with ease, and thereby avoid taking off part of the stamp or album page.

 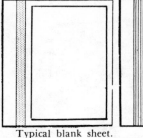 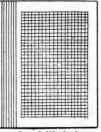

A hinge properly attached.   Typical blank sheet.   Quadrilled sheet.

When using a hinge, fold back the upper one-quarter and lightly moisten the gummed side. This part is then affixed to the top of the stamp, below the perforation. Then moisten the remaining three-quarters of the hinge and attach it to the space in the album. Be sure not to apply too much moisture. Otherwise the overflow may cause the stamp itself to adhere to the album page.

Never remove a wet hinge from your stamp or album. This is liable to make a tear or thin spot. Wait a few hours until it is perfectly dry and then it will peel off easily.

Supplementary Stamp Album

It is sometimes advisable for a collector to have another album containing blank or quadrilled pages in addition to an illustrated album. This is to take the overflow of stamps from the overcrowded regular album. This extra album can also hold new issues, oddities, unlisted varieties, stamps in pairs, strips, blocks, postmark cancellations, covers, philatelic stationery items, and other items for which there are no spacings provided in the illustrated album. It can also hold your duplicates for trading purposes.

Blank Albums

Utilized by the more advanced collectors. These come usually with either metal posts, three ring binders or spring back styles. However, sheets of the ring binders usually lay entirely flat.

Blank albums have decided advantages. Spacings for stamps or countries are not limited as in illustrated albums. This also gives a collector an opportunity to add decorative and illustrative details to the pages. There is unlimited space for variations of stamps no matter how slight, or how large in number. Pages may be plain or lightly quadrilled.

Quadrilled Printed Blank Sheets

These have both horizontal and parallel lines lightly printed across each other, forming small squares. They are especially suitable for album sheets. The squares aid in the proper and symmetrical placing of stamps.

Before Planning A Blank Album

First consider various types of borders and page decorations to be sure you choose the kind you like. This is important, because once you adopt any style you will have to retain it if you want to keep your pages looking uniform in the future. Do not utilize excess ornamentation. This may detract from the main exhibit, which is the stamps. Also, keep the items occupying a full page spread out and well-balanced. Do not crowd everything in on half a page and have the other half almost empty.

Make allowances for headings, such as countries, philatelic titles, etc. These may be hand-lettered. Allow adequate space for descriptions, as well as the symmetrical mounting of the stamps. Do not crowd too much on a page, regardless of how little the value. Plenty of space around improves the appearance. The best method of safeguarding yourself against such errors is to first plan out the layout of the page. It is advisable to make a rough sketch before acting too hastily with the execution of the work. By the use of a little headwork, you may save yourself hours of repetitious and tiresome handwork. It may be a little too advanced to mention, but good taste is important if there is under consideration the intention to use some of the sheets for entering in Philatelic Contests or Expositions.

Writing Up

Applies especially to advanced collectors in making descriptions and furnishing other informative matter regarding stamps mounted up in blank albums. Unless the collector is a gifted letterer or penman, he should avail himself of whatever ready-made titles, headings or other descriptive material he may find available in print. Gummed labels with names of countries and philatelic titles are usually on sale in booklet form in most stamp shops. Lettering outfits are usually to be found in stationery and art supply stores. In lettering, writing up, and calculating space, first do this in light pencil. This will enable corrections to be easily made before the final writing up in ink.

Some discriminating collectors go to the expense of hiring a competent letterer or having the descriptions set up in type. There are some professional letterers and layout artists who render such a service for philatelists. However, for doing these by hand, such equipment is required as a lettering outfit, lettering pens in various styles, ruling pens, India ink (black, etc.), T square, triangle rule, and drawing board.

To get best results consistently, dip the writing and ruling pens in water after use, and thoroughly dry with pieces of cloth.

Typewriting may also be utilized in writing up a collection. In this respect, the advantages of a two-color ribbon (black and red) should not be overlooked.

Typical mounts with black background. With stamps inserted.

Mounts (Pochettes)

Although a hinge may be considered a mount, this latter term in modern times usually refers to a transparent pocket (or pochette). These are usually self affixing and are available with or without black background, according to the various sizes of individual stamps, strips, pairs, blocks, etc.

Also, mounts may be cut to measure from transparent acetate tubes procurable in most popular sizes. Some are self-affixing, and others are attached by means of a special hinge. These kinds of mounts are more economical than those purchased individually.

Mounts afford better protection, as contents can be inspected with no need to touch the stamps. Also, there is no need for hinges to come into contact with the stamps, and this eliminates the possibility of thin spots or removal of gum, or other possible damage. Acetate mounts also add lustre to stamps displayed.

Considering the low cost of protective mounts it is unthinkable to diplay your more expensive and scarcer stamps by any other means.

CLASSIFICATION OF STAMP ISSUES

As with other things in our modern age of specialization, postage stamps are issued for various distinct services. Of course, the overwhelming majority of types of stamps are still printed for ordinary use. The post office also offers various other services: mail can be hastened by airpost; expedited by special delivery, registered, insured, certified, and a receipt acquired. For these various extra services there are special stamps, as there are for parcel post, collection of due postage, etc. These various classes of special stamps have an identifying letter (or key) before each of their catalog numbers in Scott's as well as in other catalogs. The major groups of these special issues are enumerated below.

Ordinary Stamp

Semi-Postal Stamp

Airpost Stamp

Ordinary Postage Stamp Issues

This refers to series of stamps for general and all-purpose postal use. To this group belong the overwhelming majority of adhesive stamps. These are distinguished from Commemorative or other stamps of special or limited use of purpose.

Semi-Postal Issues

Applies to such stamps where part or all of the receipts are given over to some charitable cause ,public welfare, or other relief fund. On some of these stamps are mentioned the amount for postage in addition to a surtax for the fund. The total of both is the price of the stamp.

Airpost Stamps

These are stamps issued for the express use of air mail matter only.

Airpost Semi-Postal Stamps

Representative of those airpost stamps that have part of their revenue (or surtax) designated for some welfare cause.

Airpost Semi-Postal Stamp

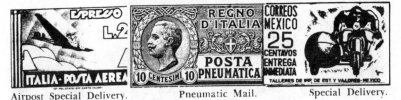

Airpost Special Delivery.   Pneumatic Mail.   Special Delivery.

Airpost Special Delivery Stamps

These stamps are used for the combined airpost and special delivery services.

Pneumatic Postage Stamps

Special stamps for enclosure of mail matter in cylinders sent through tubes by compressed air. Usually utilized for local mail within city limits.

Special Delivery Stamps

These indicate that the sender has paid an extra fee which guarantees that the letter or package will be delivered to its destination immediately upon arrival at the local post office. Otherwise it has to wait its turn along with the ordinary mail for regular delivery.

Personal Delivery Stamps

These stamps insure delivery to the addressee only. Of special value to letters of confidential or romantic content.

Authorized Delivery Stamps

For an extra charge represented by the use of such a specific stamp, the delivery of mail may be made by special private post, instead of through regular post office channels.

Registration Stamps

A special stamp for use on letters or parcels which provides for a receipt and compensation in case of loss. Ordinary postage stamps are usually acceptable for the extra charge of this service.

Insured Letter Stamps

Allows indemnity up to amount insured on mail matter covered by these special stamps.

Registration Stamp

Authorized Delivery.   Personal Delivery.   Insured Letter

Certified Mail.

Acknow. Receipt

Postage Due

Late Fee Stamp

Certified Mail Stamps

This does not allow indemnity in event of loss. The chief importance of this stamp is just to verify the mailing and delivery of a piece of mail.

Acknowledgment-Of-Receipt Stamps

Such stamps are available in some countries. If attached to a letter, the post office will notify the sender of the arrival of the message.

Postage-Due Stamps

Special stamps affixed by the post office on mail matter lacking or having insufficient postage. The amount specified is collected from the recipient. Due stamps as a general rule have a central numeral design. This is to make it convenient to collect the required amount.

Late Fee Stamps

Through use of these stamps a letter that has been mailed after normal closing time to reach train, boat, etc., will receive special messenger service to catch up with the already departed mail load. Usually designated RETARDO by Latin American countries.

Military Postage Stamps

Special stamps issued during a war for use by the armed forces of a country.

War Tax Stamps

In addition to the regular postal rate an extra amount is added as surtax to help defray war costs.

Occupation Stamps

For use by a foreign country in the occupied part of an enemy territory.

Military Stamp

War Tax Stamp

Occupation Stamp

Official Stamp.   Life Insurance   Newspaper Stamp   News. Tax Stamp

Official Postage Stamps

These stamps are for general official mail. Some countries have these stamps divided according to the various governmental departments inscribed on the stamp. For example, see U. S. 1873-79 Official Stamps. Regular postal issues are also converted into official stamps through overprints such as "Official," "Service," "O. H. M. S.", etc.

Life Insurance Department Stamps

Refers to stamps issued by New Zealand for use on mail matter of the Government Life Insurance Department.

Newspaper Stamps

Used for postage on single or bulk shipments of newspapers.

Newspaper Tax Stamps

Not to be confused with Newspaper Stamps, which are used for postage. Newspaper Tax Stamps are used strictly as a custom tax on the importation of foreign newspapers.

Parcel Post Stamps

Special stamps for use on parcels only.

Special Handling Stamps

Affixing such a special stamp to a parcel will afford it the same service as first class mail.

Parcel Post Postage-Due Stamps

For use only on parcel-post mail to indicate the extra amount to be collected on account of insufficient postage.

Postal Tax Stamps

Not valid for postage but generally used as a tax to raise funds for certain specific welfare or other purposes. These may or may not be obligatory on all mail matter over a certain period.

Parcel Post Stamp   Special Handling   Parcel Post Due   Postal Tax Stamp

THE BIRTH OF A NEW STAMP – THE STAMP DESIGN, THE MODEL, PROOFS, TRIALS AND ESSAYS

First there is government authorization for the new stamp issue which may be for regular or special use. Also other factors are to be considered before a new stamp is born. The purpose of the issue, the frame, decorations, coloring, etc., must be given due thought before proceeding with the next step of making the design.

It is unusual for one artist to do the complete art work for a design. This is usually given out to three craftsmen, each a specialist in his particular branch of art. To one will be assigned the subject of the central vignette, to another the ornamental frame and very likely a third for the lettering.

Trial or rough sketches are then submitted to postal officials in pencil, ink, etc. and in one or more colors. The final accepted drawing is known as the model.

The Model

This is the finished accepted design usually enlarged four to eight times the intended size of the stamp and is used by the engraver for guidance in the process of making the die of a stamp. Accompanying the model may be photographs to render more authenticity to the central subject. Also other helpful aids may be submitted such as supplementary drawings and suggestions on the art work, frame, lettering, coloring, etc.

Typical Die Proofs. Usually printed on fine card or India paper
with wide margins around.

The type of die depends upon what process of printing is
intended to be used.

During the course of the preparatory work of a new stamp
it may be necessary to make various trial impressions and
proof reproductions per below:

Engravers Progress Proofs

These are trial impressions taken during the course of making a die. They serve to check on the progress and make corrections.

Die Proofs

Upon completion of the die, trial printings are taken during
the progress towards acceptability. These impressions are
known as die proofs. They are final checks before the die is
impressed into the transfer roll or final plate.

Color Trials

These are experimental printings made from a die or plate
in various shades and colors before a final decision is made.
Color trials do not include those with the accepted color or
colors.

Color Proofs

Proofs made in the adopted color or colors are known as
color proofs.

Plate Proofs

The trial impressions from the printing plate before the
actual issue. They are ungummed and printed on card with
wide margins all around.

Essays

Designs which were proposed to the government for consideration as a stamp and actually printed from a plate but
which were rejected.

Various Essays.

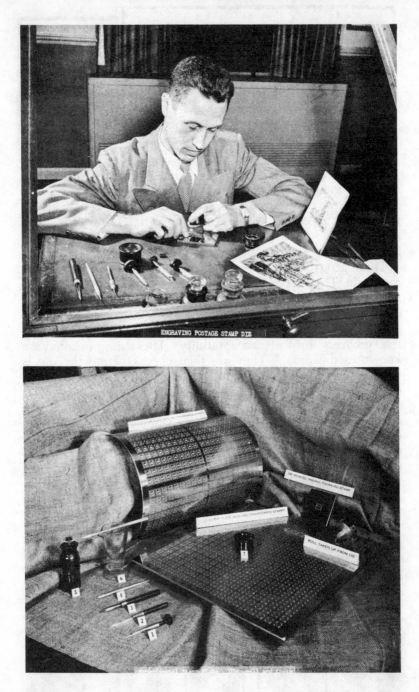

ENGRAVING POSTAGE STAMP DIE

Original Die. Transfer Roll. Flat and Cylinder Plates. Engraver's Tools: 1. Graver (or Burin); 2. Scraper; 3 Burnisher; 4. Etching Needle; 5. Mixture Etching Ground; 6. Acid Solution; 7. Engraver's vision glass.

METHODS OF PRINTING STAMPS

Among the principal methods of printing stamps are the following:

1. Recess or line engraved printing. Also known as Intaglio Method. Other forms are Photogravure (Rotogravure).
2. Relief or typography. (By means of type and blocks). Also known as Letterpress and Surface Printing.
3. Lithography (or Offset Printing).
4. Embossing.

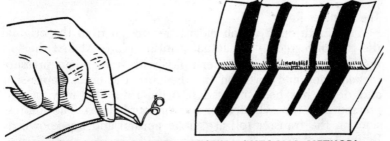

RECESS—LINE ENGRAVED PRINTING (INTAGLIO METHOD)

The best and most artistic stamps including most all U. S. Stamps have been printed by this process either through flat or cylinder plates. Engraving is a process through means of which a design is cut out of a metal plate.

During the process of printing by this method the ink flows into the crevices cut out of the plate. The normal level surface is then wiped clean thus leaving the ink only in the crevices. By pressure from the press the paper (which has been made damp) is forced into the crevices, picking up the ink. The result is that the printing will reveal only those mounds and lines of ink deposited from the aforementioned crevices on to the paper. The rest of the plate (or non printing area) having been wiped inkless, will be naturally blank in the printing.

A line engraved stamp thus has a raised and depressed surface which can often be observed through a suitable magnifier under a strong light. It is often possible to feel the irregular surface.

The Die (Line Engraved)

With the original drawing and perhaps other materials as the design, photographs, etc. as guides (see Model), a single stamp is cut out of a block of soft metal in reverse by the engraver through means of a sharp cutting instrument, known as the graver (or burin). After completion, the die is then hardened and ready for actual printing or more likely for the Transfer Roll, for use in the formation of a plate for printing sheets.

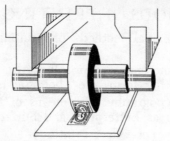

By being rocked back and forth an impression is transferred from hardened steel die below to the softened steel roller above.

The Transfer Roll

A roller through which means the design from the original die is transferred to the actual printing plate. At first the soft metal cylinder of the transfer roll is with tremendous pressure rocked back and forth on the die until the exact impression and depth has been pressed into the roll. This may be impressed into the cylinder for one or more times. The impressions in the transfer roll are made normal and are known as Relief Transfers.

The Plate (Engraved)

As the first step in making a modern engraved plate for printing sheets of stamps, the transfer roller is now hardened and by the same back and forth rocking process the one or more dies on the roll is pressed into the soft metal of the intended printing plate. Each is known as a transfer. As many transfers of these dies are reproduced on the plate as will be required for the sheet. The reproductions this time are by the same procedure as before but impressed in reverse on the plate. As final step the plate is then hardened and usually plated with a thin layer of chrome or nickel to stand heavy wear. It is now ready for the actual printing.

The Die Plate

This applies to early methods where the original engraver's die is used for the actual printing on paper. No other plate or duplicate is reproduced therefrom. There is therefore no use of the Transfer Roll.

Hand Engraved Plates

This is another throwback to early printing methods. Each of the individual dies making up the plate has been done separately by hand one at a time by the engraver, instead of being pressed out with benefit of the Transfer Roll.

No matter how skillfully executed by the human hand, there cannot fail to be some difference in hand engraved plates between one die and the other. Hence the role of the specialist in reconstructing an original sheet from single copies of stamps. (See also Reconstructed Sheets).

Typifying a short transfer.   Typifying a double transfer.

OTHER CHARACTERISTICS OF LINE ENGRAVED PRINTING

Short Transfer

This is when the Transfer Roll is not rocked its entire length during the impressing of a transfer on a plate. This results in an incomplete design on the finished plate which shows up on the printed stamp.

Double Transfer

This applies to a new plate. A stamp design having been impressed into a new plate by the transfer roll in the wrong position is corrected by removal of the unsatisfactory work and a new impression made. A double transfer is brought about if the removal of the first impression has not been complete. This will therefore result in whatever lines that have not been adequately removed showing up in the printing duplicated in part, or in whole with the old design. This term is also used in Lithography for the same reason.

Typifying a re-entry. Note old lines in FIJI and forehead.

Re-Entry

This applies to old or worn out plates where it is necessary for the re-entry (or re-use) of the Transfer Roll to re-impress the lines of the old design. Unless this is done with the utmost precision the new lines will not coincide exactly with the original lines. A variation under such a circumstance is known as a Re-entry. These are usually only detectable when comparisons are made in printings between the original plate and that after repair.

Typifying a shifted transfer.

Shifted Transfer

During the rocking back and forth of the Transfer Roll in impressing a design into the plate, the lines may not coincide due to a deviating shift of the roll from the original lines. This results in a close but noticeable duplication of some of the features.

To left the original design and to right the re-engraved design.
Note change in frame (as enlarged).

Re-Engraved (or Re-Cutting)

This denotes an extensive alteration, deepening or strengthening of lines of an old die or plate by hand tool. This brings about noticeable variations between the original and adjoining impressions of the stamps. New printings of stamps having changes brought on under the aforementioned circumstances are considered as re-engraved.

To left the stamp from original die shows worn details. To right the retouched die shows strengthening of lines and details.

Retouched

Indicates that only slight alterations or improvements have been made on the details of a die or plate but not as extensive as in re-engraving or re-cutting.

LARGE ROTARY PRESS

Photogravure (Rotogravure)

Other forms of recess printing sometimes found in stamps are *photogravure* and *rotogravure.* In both processes, an original illustration is reproduced by photo-mechanical means. Prints are obtained from a plate or cylinder upon which the design is etched below the surface. The amount of ink deposited on the paper is determined not by cross-hatching of lines as in line-engraving, but by the depth of the cells in the printing plate. The deeper the cell, the more ink it holds and the darker the impression on the paper. Gravure printing can be identified, with the aid of a strong magnifying glass, by the presence of these cells which appear as evenly distributed dots throughout the design. It is important to be able to distinguish the dots of gravure from halftone dots, which will be described in the section on relief printing.

Specimen printed by Photogravure (Rotogravure) process.

Rotogravure Printing

A more modern method of photogravure printing through means of rotary (cylinder) plates.

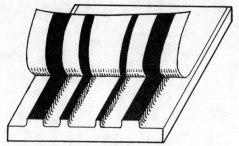

Principle of typographed printing (in relief). The printing surface is elevated in reverse to being cut out of the plate as in recess (Intaglio) method

TYPOGRAPHY (IN RELIEF)

Also known as letterpress or surface printing. Typography as its name indicates is printing by means of type and blocks. It is a very common and frequently used process especially with commercial printers and publishers of books, newspapers and magazines.

The principles of this process are the exact reverse of recess (line engraved) printing. Whereas in the latter method the lines printed are from the crevices (ink filled) which have been carved out of the plate, in Typography the printing is from the raised surface above the level of the non-printing area of the plate (in relief). The printing is entirely flat with no elevations of ink to be observed or felt as in line engraving. However, lines from the pressure of the press can sometimes be observed on the back of the typographed stamps. An ordinary rubber stamp is an excellent example of relief printing. Upon examination you will notice the characters to be impressed as raised.

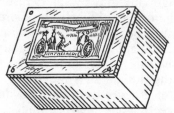

A block (or cut) used for typographic printing.

Type Set Printing (Typography)

Instead of a solid die or plate, the design and reading matter of a stamp is made up of type, rules and ornaments usually to be found in a printer's shop.

The Die (Typography)

As can be ascertained from previous paragraphs the process of making a die for typography or surface printing is in reverse to line engraving. In this method the lines and details of the stamps stand out with the rest of the die cut away.

Typical examples of type-set stamps.

The Mould (Matrices)

A corresponding and exact impression in either wax, plaster of Paris, papier-mache or other suitable material taken from an original die and which is used as a means of casting therefrom metal reproductions or cliches.

Stereos

Into a mould there is deposited molten metal as copper, nickel, etc. and from which stereos are casted. As many stereos can be made as are required. They are then assembled together to make the printing plate. To endure more wear, stereos can be plated with chromium or other hard metals.

Electrotyping

This is a more modern and improved method than stereotyping. By this process, reproductions of a die or plate are made which avoids the use and wearing out of the originals. A wax, lead, plaster, gutta-percha or other suitable material is first made from the original die either in recess or in relief. Into this a thin plate of molten copper is electrically deposited to the required thickness. When removed from the mould it will be an exact copy of the die. This is repeated as many times as required. These (cliches or electros in reverse) are usually strengthened and mounted on a block to a required height and used separately or locked together to form a plate. For extra heavy duty these cliches may be plated with chromlum or nickel.

Other examples of stamps by process of typography.

Cliche

Refers to an individual stereo or an electro or may apply to any unit of stamps making up a plate for printing purposes. A number of these may be locked together to form a printing plate.

Setting—Resetting

An arrangement of movable type to form a printing plate. Resetting denotes the re-arrangement of the separate pieces or cliches of which a plate is composed.

By Half Tone Process. Note finer details.

Half Tone Process

In engraving a process of making a printing plate or block through photography. The subject is reproduced by dots caused by interposing a glass screen of closely drawn vertical and horizontal lines between the camera and the object. This breaks up the illustration into small dots. The film taken is then developed and a print made upon a sensitized copper or zinc plate. The print is next developed (or etched) which by this process have the parts not affected by the light removed and leaves the remaining part that contains the design to remain and become the desired plate (or block). Where the dots are closely spaced the printing will be dark. Where they are wide apart, the printing will be light.

By Line Process. Note more solid lines and background.

Line Blocks

This process is similar to the half tone process except that no screen is used during the photographing of the subject. The result is that the design will be made up of solid metal lines instead of fine dots.

Double Strike

Applies to electrotypes or stereotypes whereby part or the whole of the design is impressed twice. This is caused by a shift during the implanting of the die upon the mould from which the plate is made.

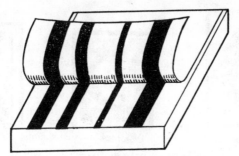

Lithography is based on the principle that grease and water repels each other.

LITHOGRAPHY

Lithographed printing is a process originally through stone plates. However, the more modern Lithography now makes use also of aluminum and zinc plates. The printing generally looks crude and the details not as sharp as in engraved or typographed printing. It is this dullness and also its extreme flatness on both sides of the stamps that distinguishes Lithography. The printing is based upon the principle that grease and water repel each other. There are absolutely no elevations or depressions which influence the printing. The impressions are entirely flat. The stamp design is first impressed, photographed or transplanted in reverse to the stone or metal plate from a prepared paper with drawing in a special greasy ink with acid to eat away those portions not covered by the ink. The inked details then adhere to the stone surface and by a chemical process are prevented from spreading over to the non-inked parts. The stone or plate is next wetted by a watering roller. Whereas the moisture is absorbed by the blank (greaseless) spaces it is rejected by the greasy inked lines of the design. Other rollers next apply the ink but is thereupon repelled by the watered parts and absorbed by the greased parts making up the design, which finally as part of the process is transferred to the paper as a printed impression.

Photo-Lithography (Offset Printing)

The modern equivalent of lithography is photo-lithography (or photo-offset). It has its designs or subjects etched into a plate of aluminum or zinc which is then bent into cylinder form. The originals are transferred to the plate by photomechanical means. This plate while revolving on the press receives its ink from inking rollers and in turn transfers a reversed or offset impression on to another cylinder with a blanket of vulcanized rubber. The latter cylinder next contacts the paper and upon which it makes normal printed impressions.

Typical examples of Embossed Stamps.

EMBOSSING

This process is used most commonly for stamps printed directly on envelopes. The design is embossed directly onto the paper by pressure from a die pressed against the opposite side. This creates a raised area on the front of the envelope. This raised area, usually consisting of the design or portrait, is often surrounded by color. The ink must, of course, be applied from the top. It can be seen that embossing is usually a process requiring two dies operating simultaneously; one supplying ink coverage from the top and the other forcing the colorless raised surface up from the bottom.

PAPER

This is a very important factor in the manufacture of stamps. There are hundreds of kinds but we are only concerned with those specifically used in the printing of stamps. The basic substances of paper are wood pulp and water. The better grades also utilize cotton, linen, rags and other fibrous materials. All these are treated, bleached and beaten to a mash or pulp. After the water is drained out, a sheet of moist paper is produced.

Dandy Roll

This is a roller with a wire mesh attached which impresses itself upon the paper pulp as it leaves the vat and gives the paper its inside pattern known as wove or laid. The amount of pressure on the wet pulp determines the thickness of the paper. Upon the roll are attached the "bits" which press the watermark into the paper through making its form thinner in the paper.

BEHREND METHOD (making watermarks)

Another method besides the dandy roll for making watermarks is the high speed method invented by Ernst R. Behrend, one of the founders of the Hammermill Paper Co. The design in soft rubber on a revolving wheel, indents by pressure the watermark into the underside of the sheet of paper. (see illustration)

A huge paper machine called the Fourdrinier. It is one of the largest single pieces of mechanism. Fully equipped its cost is more than two million dollars. The dandy roll is indicated thereon.

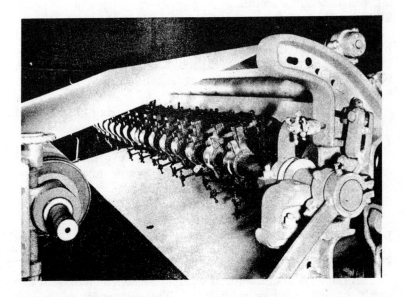

BEHREND METHOD. The watermark is impressed while the paper is largely water. During operation more water is squeezed out but watermark remains.

Bank note paper.   Burele surfaced paper.

VARIOUS PAPERS USED FOR STAMPS

Bank Note Paper
Stamps printed on back of unfinished bank notes due to paper shortage.

Batonne Wove Paper
Not much in use. Has watermarks of long light lines running far apart in plain wove paper. See Mexico 1867-8 and Afghanistan 1880-8.

Batonne Laid Paper
Has laid lines running between the long lines of the Batonne wove paper.

Blue Paper
Due to experimenting with paper containning large rag content. Noticeable on some of the U.S. 1908-9 Issues including the Lincoln Memorial.

Blued (or Bleute) Paper
Although not intended to be blue, this paper has turned blue because of the chemical reaction of the paper and ink used. See Great Britain 1841 1d red, Cape of Good Hope 1853, Nova Scotia 1851 and New Brunswick 1851.

Bond Paper
A more durable and tough grade of paper. Rag fibre is used in its manufacture. Usually watermarked.

Burele Surfaced Paper (or Burelage)
Has a network of lines and dots. Usually printed in color on the face or back of stamps for protection against re-use. See Estonia 1928-35 and Venezuela 1932-8.

Card
Stamps printed on cardboard. Usually used also as coins. Good examples of these are Russia 1915 Romanoff issue and Austria 1920 Issue.

Chalky (Chalk Surfaced) Paper
This paper is manufactured with a coating of chalk that can easily be dissolved or rubbed off. This prevents removal of cancellation. See also coated paper. For examples see British Guiana 1905-7 and Jamaica 1905, ½p.

Coated (or Surfaced) Paper

Denotes a paper with a coating which may be by chalk, enamel or other chemically produced substances, varnish, etc., and whose surface including the design will dissolve when any effort is made to wash off the cancellation for re-use. Care should therefore be taken in handling these stamps around water.

Colored Paper

The fabric of this paper is colored throughout, impregnating both surfaces. This should not be confused with surface-colored paper to which color is applied on one side but is not part of the inside texture. See Austria-Offices in Turkey, 1913-4.

Dickinson Paper

Named after its inventor, John Dickinson. It has long silk threads imbedded into the texture. Any effort to remove a cancellation will loosen the threads and cut the paper. Examples of this are Great Britain 1847-54, Switzerland 1854-62 and Bavaria 1849-68.

Double Paper

Consists of two sheets pasted together. The two sheets separate when any attempt is made to wash off the cancellation. This is not to be confused with rotary press double paper.

Enameled Paper

Has an extra heavy coating of clay, which gives a polished enameled surface. The purpose is to prevent the use of the stamp again as well as to offer a bright and glossy appearance.

Granite Paper (short threads)

Granite Paper (Silurian)

Similar to silk paper except that the colored silky fibres in the granite paper are too small to be distinguished as threads. See Switzerland 1905 and after; also Austria 1890-1906.

Laid Paper

Map Paper

Moire Paper

Hard (Wove) Paper
This is of special significance in identifying the United States postage and official stamps issued by the Continental Bank Note Company issue of 1873-5. This paper is often tested by holding the bottom of the stamp with one hand while striking the upper part repeatedly with a finger of the other hand. If the paper is hard it will usually snap back firmly and rigidly. If held to the light the inside texture will be found to be much more closely woven than that of soft porous paper.

India Paper
A thin tough paper which usually gives fine impressions. It is used extensively for proofs and for large books where it is desirable to limit the over-all bulk.

Laid Paper
Will reveal parallel lines close together across the stamps when held to the light. When the lines are far apart the paper is batonne. See Latvia 1919 and Mexico 1874-81.

Manila Paper
A coarse grade of paper made of Manila hemp fibre. Often used for wrappers and low-priced envelopes. Most common color is light brown. Usually smooth on one side and coarse on the other.

Map Paper
Stamps printed on backs of military maps. This was due to a paper shortage.

Moire Paper
Has a silky pattern printed on the front or back of stamps. See Mexico 1872.

Native Paper
Made of rice grass or silk fibre. Usually of native manufacture. Of varied nature depending on the origin. Used on early issues of China, Japan and some of the native states of India.

Ribbed Paper

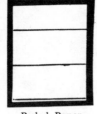
Ruled Paper

Safety Paper

Pelure Paper

A very thin, crisp and almost transparent but tough paper. May be either wove or laid texture. The term is French and means onion peel. See Estonia 1920-4 and Russia 1921.

Porous Paper

Of soft porous texture. It lacks firmness and, when held to the light the porous and sparse inside texture offers little resistance. See also soft paper.

Quadrille Watermarked Paper

Watermarked paper having both horizontal and parallel lines forming squares or rectangles.

Ribbed Paper

The texture of this paper has corrugations like ribs running across paper. See first issues of Austria and Austria-Lombardy Venezia.

Rotary Press Double Paper

This is caused by a break in paper during printing on a rotary press, when the end of a continuous paper roll is reached and has to be connected with a new roll. The printing operation is continued by overlapping and glueing both ends together. Stamps printed on the pasted-together part are known as Rotary Double Press Varieties. Usually these are destined for the waste basket, but sometimes they escape detection and are sold through the post office.

Ruled Paper

Paper printed with faint, parallel colored lines similar to that in writing paper. See Latvia 1919 and Mexico 1887.

Safety (or Security) Paper

Has a blue tint. Any attempt to remove a cancellation will discolor the paper as well as possibly wipe off the design as well. Used by Great Britain on 4d stamp of 1855. See also Venezuela 1932 Airport Issue.

Silk Paper (Long threads)

Wove Paper

Silk Paper

This has fibres looking like silk threads in body of stamp. These are especially to.be observed on many of the old U.S. Revenue Stamps of 1862-81 Issues. Another paper, similar to silk paper is granite paper except that the silky fibres in granite paper are too small to be distinguished as threads. Also see Switzerland 1854-62.

Soft or Porous Paper

It is by such a paper that we will be able to recognize U.S. Postage and Official stamps printed by the American Bank Note Co. 1879 Issue. In comparison with the hard paper as described heretofore, it is quite thicker and lacks rigidity and snap. If held to the light there will be revealed many coarse blemishes and crude dots. These comparisons of hard and soft paper per above are important as there were U.S. Postage and Official Stamps printed in 1873 to 1879 which were exactly alike except in these differences of paper.

Surface Colored Paper

This paper is colored on one side only. The other side has the natural untinted color of the paper. See France 1876-90 and Austria-Offices in Turkey 1908.

Tinted Paper

Refers to a slight or faint coloring of the paper of a stamp. Also relates to the differences in the shades of the color.

Varnished Paper

Similar to chalky or coated paper. Has small bars or other figures of varnish on the surface before printing the design of the stamp. Soaking the stamps to remove the cancellation causes the varnish and the ink to come off. See Austria 1901 and 1905. Also Russia 1909-12.

Wove Paper

This is the main type of paper used for printing stamps. It is usually very smooth on both surfaces and if held to the light will be found to have a well finished, uniform texture. It is easy to examine a sample of this paper as all current U.S. stamps are printed on wove stock.

Ink Manufacturing and Testing Division

COLOR AND SHADES

It is difficult to find a field where there are a larger variety of colors involved than in Philately. There are no standard catalogs that generally agree on colors. Disagreements may be found in any catalog itself depending upon the opinions of the different authors making up the contents and descriptions. Also many of the shades listed in catalogs are questioned as unnecessary. A good number of these shades were due on the amount of ink used in the printing pressure against the paper, chemical reactions, reprinting of issues, etc. Also age, sunlight and other exposures, deficient eyesight, artificial light, colors in pairs and groups, etc. can distort or mislead the proper identification of colors. Also stamps are deliberately treated to change color for the purpose to defraud. Nevertheless to distinguish color is of the utmost importance no matter how minor or to what slight a degree. For instance, an unused copy of United States 1881-2 issue, 10c brown, is valued by Scott's for $12.00 whereas the exact same stamp in black brown is valued at $50 00. Color is a topic that is best left to the experience and discretion of the collector, with the aid of a reliable color guide and Scott's catalog.

First stamp is normal. The other stamp has central design with different color printed upside down. This is known as an invert.

Bi-Colored Stamps

Denotes stamps printed in two colors. The central portion or design of the stamp is usually in one color, and the frame, ornamentation and inscriptions in one or more other colors. Due to there being at least two printings required, the central portion may be sometimes printed upside down by mistake. This is known as an invert which usually brings a high premium in its realization value.

Changeling

This implies that the original color of a stamp has been changed. This may be accidental or brought on by exposure, age or chemical reactions of paper and ink contents. Or it may be the result of a downright deliberate attempt to defraud.

Fugitive Colors

Colors on a stamp which will dissolve if an effort is made by applying a liquid for the express purpose of removing the cancellation.

Caution — Relating To Color

Special caution should be exercised in soaking stamps in water to wash off attached paper. This should cause concern for all surface coated stamps, as well as others that are apt to dissolve printed surface or change in color, shade or paper content. Consult list of papers elsewhere in this book as well as in Scott's Catalog. Also do not expose stamps to sunlight for any sustained period, as this may discolor the stamps or remove the colors entirely. This is often occasioned by having unprotected during sunlight, displays of stamps in shop windows.

Tints (or Shades)

The various degrees in strength or depths of a color.

Oxidized (or Sulphuretted)

Mostly due to age, exposure and chemical changes in the ink, stamps become oxidized and change color. Good examples are the early Great Britain penny stamps which were originally red and are now frequently found in almost black or dark brown. Their original color is usually restored if peroxide of hydrogen is applied to the stamp.

SEPARATION OF STAMPS

Imperforated Stamps

Imperforated Stamps are not provided with any means of separation and therefore have to be cut apart with scissors. etc. Most of these are from the early issues when machines to separate stamps had not yet been developed. Imperforated stamps should be preferred where its margins are wide enough to eliminate any doubt that it was originally a perforated stamp. It is considered a dishonest practice to convert perforated stamps into more valuable imperforated stamps by trimming off perforations. A sure way to eliminate any concern is to acquire imperforates in pairs showing this feature.

The Separation of Stamps

It was an Irishman, Henry Archer, who in 1847 invented the first method of separating stamps by what is known as the roulette process. At a later date he improved on this with a new machine which made small holes all around the stamps which are known as perforations.

Pair with "imperforate between" condition. The pair to right has missing (or blind) perforations.

Imperforate Between

Denotes a pair or more of stamps whereby through mechanical error there is lacking normal perforations between two rows of stamps. This condition may be either vertical or horizontal.

Blind Perforations

Due to faulty or worn out perforation machinery the holes may not be pierced through and instead there may be visible just mere impresses on the paper. Such indentations on the paper are considered blind perforations.

Perforated Stamps

Perforated Stamps are provided with means of separation through the little holes around them as you see almost every day on the ordinary postage stamps. There are different sizes of perforations. These are usually measured by the Perforation Gauge according to the number within its width of two centimetres of space. This is very simple. Just run the edge of your stamp along the gauge until the dots fit exactly into the perforations. You will then find the correct figure printed at that point on the gauge. If the figure is 12, for instance, it means that there are 12 perforations within the two centimetres of space as described heretofore. This is important as there may be stamps exactly alike except for the difference in perforation measurements and this may also mean a great difference in dollars and cents.

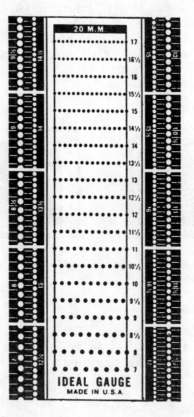

The Perforation Gauge

A measure for ascertaining the number of perforations of a stamp within two centimetres (or 20mm.) of space. The above illustrated gauge is suitable for use.

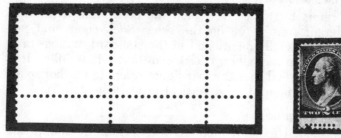

Clean Cut perforations.   Double perforations

Clean Cut Perforations (Common Perforations)

Whereby the holes or perforations of a stamp are cleanly cut through with no remnants of paper remaining. This is present in the regular U. S. stamps in which modern perforation machinery has been utilized.

Double Perforations

If the perforation machine by accident makes two impressions slightly apart the result is a double perforation. This may also be caused by a perforation machine going over a sheet twice for a correctionary purpose and which may result in two close rows of perforations.

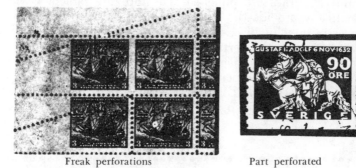

Freak perforations   Part perforated

Freak Perforations

Caused by a corner or part of a sheet being accidentally folded over so that the perforating machine impresses a diagonal, odd or inncorrect perforation. If noticed, sheets containing such freak perforations are usually removed as waste paper by the government printing staff.

Part Perforated Stamps

These stamps are perforated on the top and bottom or on the sides. The other sides are imperforated. This feature is also characteristic of coil stamps.

Compound Perforations

This refers to stamps on which the horizontal perforations are different from those on the sides. Such compound perforations are usually mentioned in the standard catalogs or in the more advanced albums as for instance 11 x 10½. It is usually understood that the first figure refers to the horizontal and the latter figure to the vertical measurement.

Perforation Processes

The principal modern methods for perforating stamps are by means of the comb perforation machine, guillotine perforating machine, the Harrow perforation machine and a device for rotary perforations.

The principle of the Comb Perforator. The dots represent the punches.

The Comb Perforator

A means of punching the top and all vertical perforation holes of one or more rows of stamps at a time. This is continued until all rows are punched. The top row punched will automatically provide the bottom row for the preceding row. A last extra punch will be required to put the bottom holes on the last row with the vertical perforations going through the lower margin of the sheet down to the bottom. The more modern comb machine perforates two rows at a stroke and is referred to as a double comb perforator; the triple perforator impresses three rows at a time.

Guillotine Method. Punches one line of perforations at a time.

The Guillotine Perforator

A perforation machine which makes only single line perforations. To distinguish line perforations from comb perforations a collector must look at the corners of stamps. In a comb perforation each hole is separated from each other whereas in line perforations the holes may go over each other where the horizontal and vertical lines of perforations cross each other.

The Harrow Perforator

Perforates at one time an entire sheet or pane of stamps.

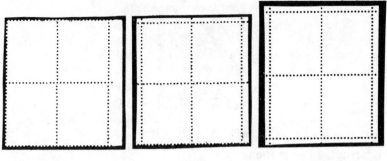

| Comb | Guillotine | Harrow |

DIFFERENCES BETWEEN THE COMB, GUILLOTINE AND HARROW PERFORATIONS

COMB: Where lines cross, the vertical perforations are slightly out of line. This occurs usually when a new row of perforations have been applied by the comb. GUILLOTINE: The single lines of horizontal and vertical perforations unevenly cross each other. HARROW: All the perforations are evenly balanced throughout the entire sheet as well as in all the corners.

Rotary Stamp Perforator

A process of making perforations in sheets or rolls by revolving wheels. This is operated first in one direction and then in the other direction.

The above stamp reflects the condition known as "interrupted (or syncopated) perforations."

Interrupted Perforations

Also known as syncopated perforations. Caused by some of the punches of the Comb perforator being missing the corresponding holes. The removal of some of the perforating blades of the comb may also be deliberate in order to overcome weakness of a paper which would if completely perforated.

Misplaced Perforations

Where the perforations holes pass through the wrong part of a stamp.

Pin or Sewing Machine Perforations

Also known as percé en points. These are in reality roulettes as the paper is only pierced and not removed. See roulettes.

Square Perforations

Small square holes usually close together as distinguished from the round shaped kind.

Private perforation for mechanical mailing machine.

Vending and Mailing Machine Perforations

Also known as private perforations. Not official but made private from imperforate sheets or roll for use in vending and office mailing machines.

Electric Eye

An electric device used to guide the perforating machine in making correct margins. A series of colored dashes in the margins aids the device in its operation.

Hyphen Hole Perforations

Of long rectangular shape similar to the hyphen mark. For examples see U. S. Revenue Issue.

ROULETTED STAMPS

Rouletted stamps like perforated stamps have means of separation but instead of having holes made through removal of paper from body of stamps it has instead incisions. These are made without removal of paper.

Perce´

In describing the various kinds of rouletting the French term percé is often adopted. This means pierced and in some instances may also indicate perforated.

Arc Roulette

(In French, percé en arc). In the shape of an arch. The incisions or cuts in this type of roulette are of semi-circular shape.

Diamond (or Lozenge) Roulette

(In French, percé en croix or perce en losanges). Roulettes in rows and shapes of XXX and usually resembling diamonds or lozenges.

Line Roulette (Ordinary)

Where the roulettes are in the shape of straight cuts of various sizes and distances between.

Oblique Roulette

(In French, perce en lignes obliques.) Roulettes with short slanting and parallel cuts.

Pin Roulette

Also incorrectly known as pin perforation or sewing machine perforations. (In French, percé en points). This is a roulette that is point-pierced but with no paper removed.

Rouletted

This is the regular name for line roulette. (In French, percé en lignes). This is a plain roulette which appears in the form of short straight cuts in lines.

Roulette In Color

(In French, percé lignes de couleur). This is accomplished during the printing of stamps. The incisions are made into the paper by use of a sharp edged and a deeper penetrating part of the printing plate which inks the cuts at the same time they are made.

Sawtooth Roulette (Serrated)

(In French percé en scie). The cuts resemble the teeth of a saw. The teeth form triangles compared to the rounded edges of, for instance, the arc and other roulettes.

Serpentine Roulette

(In French percé en serpentine). Cuts of this type are shaped in high curved wavy lines, of sinuous winding form like serpent; hence the name.

Sewing Machine Roulette

Although these have been in fact made by means of a sewing machine as in the case of Tibet 1933 Issue, some of the U. S. 2nd Issue Revenues, and the Colombia 1902-3 Barranquilla Issues, most of the so described sewing machine roulettes (or Perforations) are incorrect and are in reality pin rouletted. Some of the latter may look like sewing machine stitches but are really point pierced without use of the aforementioned machine.

Zig Zag Roulette

In French, perce´ en pointes, where cuts produce sharp turns and angles along edges of the stamps. In a zig zag course.

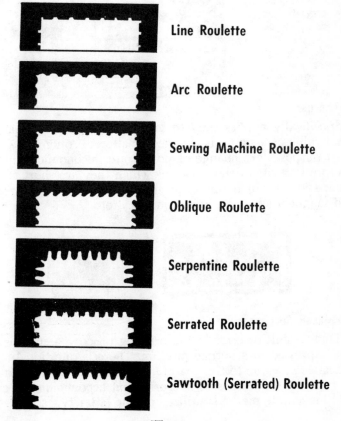

Line Roulette

Arc Roulette

Sewing Machine Roulette

Oblique Roulette

Serpentine Roulette

Serrated Roulette

Sawtooth (Serrated) Roulette

OVERPRINTS, PROVISIONALS AND SURCHARGES

OVERPRINTS AND PROVISIONALS

Some examples of Overprints (or Provisionals).

These refer to finished stamps which have other matter overprinted on them, usually for emergency purposes until a regular or new issue is printed. These may be due to economy measures, change of government, occupation in war, overturn of ruler (defacing his portrait) and most any other purpose except where the face value of a stamp is altered or changed. The latter group belong to the family of Surcharges.

Surcharges

Specifically applies only to an overprint whereby the original value of a stamp is changed or altered. Among the principal purposes are change of postal rates, economical such as overprinting such denominations which they are short of over those stamps which there are an excess of. Also to currency and language changes, war occupancy, etc.

Misplaced Surcharges

Due to shift or error in the printing process, a surcharge is not impressed in a normal position. There is questionable significance or value to this feature, if it applies to handstamped or type set surcharges or overprints on account of the crude and inaccurate methods utilized on the latter types.

Punched Overprint

The purpose of these is the same as the regular overprints but are punched (perforated) into the stamp instead of printed on it. An example is Australia punched OS.

Double Overprint or Surcharge

Indicates that the overprint or surcharge has by error been printed twice over the face of the stamp.

Handstamped Overprint

Applied by use of a handstamp. Due to this crude hand method an abundance of these overprints will usually be found to be stamped in all sorts of positions and thereby the value of these particular varieties are not considered in most cases any higher than those in normal position.

Inverted Overprint

This is brought about by the overprint being applied by the press on the sheet in upside down position.

Type Set Overprints

In such instances the overprints are set in type and as many overprints have to be set as there are stamps to the sheet. One of the results is that all these overprints may not be exactly alike. Uusually done during an emergency the chance for misspelling, omission, and incorrect letters, etc. on some of the varieties are quite likely. Especially where undertaken by a small printing shop, some letters may be substituted for others when the limited supply is used up. For examples see Nicaragua and Panama. These type set overprints are aside from those done also by the more modern and accurate processes through plates, format of cliches and printed over the sheet of stamps.

TYPICAL TYPE-SET ERRORS IN SHEET

*COLUMBIAN REPUBLIC, SANTANDER, 1907

Sheet of #67 (with errors #67a and #67b). (Find them below.)

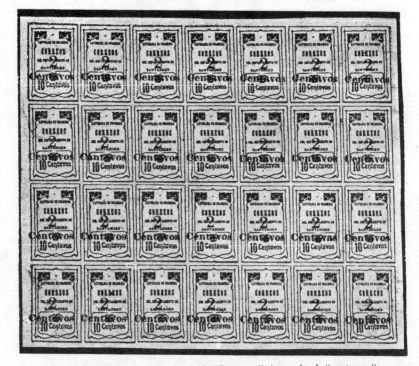

ERROR—No. 67a: Surcharged "Cantavos" instead of "centavos."
Found on second row—2nd stamp.

ERROR—No. 67b: Surcharged "Centavas" instead of "centavos."
Found on third row—6th stamp.

WATERMARKS

Watermarks are figures or designs which may be observed in a stamp just as you would see the trademark or brand name of paper by holding it to the light. Their purpose is largely as protection against duplication of the same paper. Some watermarks can be seen with ease on the back of stamps but others are more difficult to observe and require the use of a watermark detector. The most frequent watermarks are stars, crowns, letters, lines, symbols, etc.

Watermarks are impressed into the paper during the course of its manufacture. It is done by a process of making thinner in the wet paper pulp the form of the watermark by pressure from an attached wire or metal device (the bit) on the dandy roll. The latter is a revolving cylinder used in the manufacture of paper. Also see the Behrend method on pages 40-41.

A close up view of the Dandy Roll.

The Watermark Detector

This is a black tray (preferably glass) for the purpose of detecting watermarks. After having the stamp face downward in the watermark detector, pour in enough drops of Benzine to entirely cover it. This usually will reveal any watermark if in the stamp. As benzine is inflammable, non-inflammable Carbona may be used as a substitute. NOTE: These fluids should not be used for photogravure stamps or those printed with fugitive inks.

Among the various types of watermarks are the following:

Network   Honeycomb   Circles

Background Watermarks

This refers to that group of watermarks having a closely knitted pattern covering the entire width and length of a stamp. Examples are the lozenges and network watermarks of Germany. Also the honeycomb watermarks of Danzig.

Continuous Watermarks

A repetition of letters, words, symbols, etc. but of which only a part will appear on any single stamp. Brazil offers good examples of this type.

Double Line Watermarks

The watermark appears in double line lettering. Used for U. S. Stamps during 1895-1910 Issues.

Single Line Watermark

Watermark appears in single line lettering. Used among U. S. Stamps 1910-16 Issues.

Group Watermarks

Watermarks which because of their large size extend over a sizeable group of stamps.

Singular Watermarks
This is where only one complete watermark is to be found in each stamp.

Multiple Watermark
The design appears in a group or so close together that several watermarks may be seen in one stamp.

Script Watermark
The lettering or words are slanted and similar to handwriting.

Inverted Watermark
Upside down in relation to the normal position of the stamp.

Lozenge Watermark
A watermark in the shape of a lozenge. For good and noticeable examples of these see Germany 1921-22 Issues.

Opaque Watermark
This is made in reverse to the usual process of having the paper thinner due to the design of the watermark being impressed into the soft paper pulp. An opaque watermark is due to the design instead being cut in recess into the watermark device. This results in extra paper pulp being deposited within the lines of the design. When held to the light the watermark is observed as the rest of the sheet is thinner.

Sheet Watermark

Also known as spread out Watermark. Refers to a watermark whose letters or the design spreads over the entire sheet of stamps. Hence only a small part or even none at all will be on any individual stamp.

Stitch Watermark

Not intended as a watermark but caused during the process of making paper by the stitches which join the ends of the wire band covering the dandy roll. These appear as a group of short parallel lines running across the stamp.

Impressed Watermark

Impressed after the paper has been made and therefore appears as a distinct indentation.

CANCELLATION OF STAMPS BY MUTILATION

This method of cancellation was to cut off a piece of the stamp. Practiced particularly on early issues of Afghanistan.

GUM

The substance or adhesive on the back of an unused stamp which is usually moistened to attach the stamp to the envelope.

Gum found on stamps is usually white although sometimes colored. Most governments including the United States utilize non-curling and non-cracking gum. Safe ingredients such as vegetable matter, dextrose, molasses, etc. are used in the manufacture of gum to render it absolutely safe. Gum is also important in the detection of stamp forgeries as it is very difficult to match in content, color, age, etc.

Ungummed Issues
Stamps have been and are still furnished without gum by some countries. This may be due to lack of gumming facilities or the climate. Nevertheless they are considered as mint stamps if they were originally issued without gum.

Original Gum
Usually abbreviated as O.G. Indicates that the stamps have the same original gum as when sold by the post office. When stamps are so described it is assurance that it still retains the original gum.

Regummed
This refers to stamps which have lost their original gum and have been regummed. There is really no philatelic purpose or advantage to this practice as regumming not only does not add to the value but may create suspicion on any party handling such an item. To show good faith a regummed stamp should have the notation "regummed" on the back of the stamp.

GRILLS

Grills with the grooves visible on the front.

This consists of a group of grooves impressed into the fibre of the stamp so that the cancellation ink will sink right through the stamp. The purpose of this former practice was to prevent the re-use of the stamp by washing off the cancellation.

Grills are best observed on the backs of stamps. However, these sometimes become so flattened out that they are almost unnoticeable. As some stamps without the grills are more valuable, there has been a practice of having these ironed out to defraud. However, by close examination this will nevertheless be detected.

Normal Grill   Double Grill   Split Grill

Double Grill

This is an accidental double impression on a stamp with one grill visibly overlapping the other.

Split Grill

Parts of two or more grills (or portions) impressed into the same stamp. Caused by a sheet being fed off center through the grill roller.

EXPERTIZATION SERVICE

The Philatelic Foundation, 99 Park Avenue, New York, N. Y. 10016. Those requiring this service apply to the Secretary for an application,

American Philatelic Society, P.O. Box 800, State College, Pa. 16801. All items must be submitted on forms which may be obtained from the Executive Secretary.

SHEETS, PANES, BOOKLETS AND CHARACTERISTICS
PRESS SHEETS AND ORDINARY SHEETS (PANES)

The full sized complete sheet as actually comes off the press is known as the press sheet. For example, the ordinary size U. S. Stamp comes off the press in a sheet of 400 stamps. This is then cut into four parts of 100 each. Each part is the sheet of 100 you see sold in the post office. It is also known as a pane. On larger size stamps as Commemoratives, the quantities would be proportionately half of the aforementioned.

Miniature Sheets
Applies to single stamps in a sheet of a small or reduced quantity to that of the regular sheet. Has no specific commemorative purpose. It usually has large margins with or without inscriptions. Miniature sheets may also be of a special size for an emergency or for convenience in handling.

Souvenir Sheets

Issued in celebration of some exhibition, event, etc. May have one or more stamps. Around the margins or other parts of these sheets will be usually found descriptive printed matter relating to the occasion. Prospective sales from stamp exhibitions and other philatelic events have inspired many of these issues.

1890 Issue. Arrow without guide line.   1918 Issue. Arrow with guide line.

Arrows (V-Shaped Marks)

Refers to U. S. 1870-1894 stamps. Arrows found in margins of some sheets were used in place of lines in order to guide those cutting full press sheets into panes or other desired fractions. Since 1894 guide lines with arrows at both ends of the full sheets have been used on flat plate printing.

Reconstructing Sheets

Applies to plates where the die and transfer roll were not used to impress exact duplicate designs into the soft metal plate during the process of manufacture. The engraver instead made the design the required number of times by hand. Stamps printed from plates having such individually engraved stamps do not fail to have some slight variations between each other. Hence the specialist who reconstructs the original plate from the proper single copies. See also Plating.

Center Lines

These are horizontal or vertical lines as guide in dividing a sheet of stamps.

Guide Lines

These are horizontal or vertical lines (colored) on the sheets to aid in correctly perforating the stamps and the separation of the sheet into panes.

Margin of Sheet

The margin or edge bordering the stamps on the sheets. This may contain printed matter on same as name of printer, government bureau, plate number or other inscriptions.

Marginal Inscriptions

Any printed matter appearing on the margins of sheets or panes.

Gutter

The two wide spaces running vertically and horizontally through the center and dividing the sheets into panes.

Plate Numbers

For identification purposes. The numbers that usually appear on one or more of the margins of sheets or panes.

Names on Sheets

Refers to the names of countries appearing on the margins of the sheets. A good example is the U. S. 1943-44 Overrun Countries issue.

Booklets and Booklet Panes

Some governments furnish stamps in a small booklet for the convenience of the public. These may consist of one or more denominations. There are usually six stamps to a pane (or booklet sheet) which may be either in tete beche or se tenant positions.

Accidentally printed on reverse side.

Printed on Both Sides

This is a sheet of stamps printed by mistake on both sides instead of one side only.

The Expert Committee of the Philatelic Foundation at work

71

PAIRS, STRIPS AND BLOCKS

Pair

Two unseparated stamps, used or unused.

Tete-Beche Pair

This usually refers to an unseparated pair where one stamp is upside down next to another in normal position. It is necessary to keep these stamps in pairs to bring out this feature. Breaking up the pair would obviously destroy the tete-beche relationship.

Se Tenant

Refers to a pair or any group of stamps in which there are at least two varieties in unseparated condition. These are usually found in the handy size postage books sold by the post office.

Strip

A horizontal or vertical row of three or more unseparated stamps.

Bi-Lingual Pair

This is an unsevered pair where the language on one stamp is different from that of the other. Good examples of these can be found in Union of South Africa and South West Africa.

Line Pair

A pair of stamps with the guide line between.

Paste Up Pair

Refers to a pair on which appears the pasted up junction of the two sheets of flat plate printing joined for making coil stamps.

Joint Line Pair

A paste-up pair with the line in between.

Block of Stamps

An unsevered group of stamps at least two stamps wide by two stamps deep. This a block of four. Larger blocks are indicated by the number of stamps within the block.

Arrow Block

This is a block of stamps which contains in the margin a V-shaped mark sometimes referred to as an arrow. See also Arrows and Guide Lines.

Corner Block

A block of stamps taken from the corner of the complete sheet with the margins on two sides intact.

Center Line Block

A block of stamps taken from the center of a large sheet on which the crossing of the vertical and horizontal guide lines in the middle is visible.

Gutter Block

When the two wide gutter spaces cross through the center, the group is known as a Center gutter block. See Gutter for illustration of typical block.

Plate Number Blocks

A block of stamps bearing that margin of the sheet on which is printed the plate number.

Imprint Block

A block of four or more stamps of sufficient length to include the entire margin imprint of the sheet.

Name Blocks

For illustration see Names on Sheets.

COILS

Usually supplied in rolls by the government so that they may be used in labor saving and vending machines. May be perforated either horizontally or vertically.

Coil Plate Numbers

These are intended to be cut off in the process of making coil sheets. Consequently they are very scarce and are found only when by accident the sheets have been cut off center.

Privately perforated coils for use in labor saving and vending machines.

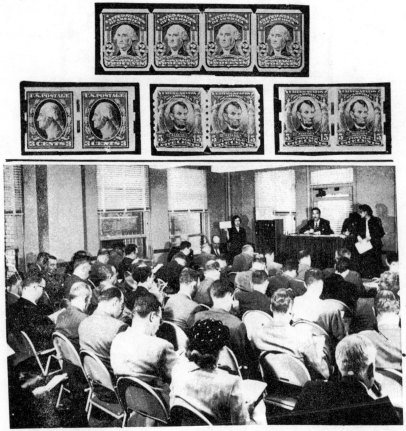

View of H. R. Harmer's Public Auction

ERRORS AND INVERTS

Sometimes an error occurs in the printing of stamps such as mis-spelling, omission of letters from word, wrong color, incorrect amounts, watermark in wrong position, errors in engraving etc. It may be almost anything. True philatelists are always on the lookout for these, as such errors usually command high premiums. Many of the rarest stamps are due to some mistake in printing. There is also a class of errors called inverts. This happens in bi-colored (two colored) stamps. The central picture or design may be printed upside down by mistake.

Some Famous Errors in Stamps

THE MAURITIUS ERRORS. The first two stamps of the 1847 Issue were engraved Post Office instead of Post Paid. The result is that these stamps are worth between $15,000 to $20,000 each.

Valuable Mauritius 1945 cover with copy each of rare 1¢ and 2¢ POST OFFICE errors. Acquired by Weill Bros. of New Orleans for $78,400.

24c U.S. 1918 AIRPOST STAMP WITH INVERT.
A single copy of this stamp was sold for $47,000. (see page 88)

Errors in Color

These are accidental printings in an incorrect color as for instance, where a 2c stamp is printed blue instead of its usual red. However, care should be exercised in accepting such finds as the colors of stamps can be changed by exposure to sunlight, chemicals, fumes, etc. Genuine errors in color are very rare.

77

Errors in Overprints

These are pretty common. Usually brought on due to emergency and haste. These may occur through errors in typesetting, mis-spelling, missing or broken letters, punctuation, inverted words, spacing, wrong positions, insufficient type, etc. Care should be exercised before accepting any as bona fide errors as some of these may be due to poor printing or worn out type instead of actual mistakes. Also see type-set overprints.

Imperforate Errors

This refers to stamps where the perforations are omitted accidentally. During process of perforating a line of perforations intended between two rows of stamps is omitted by error. This brings obout an imperforate condition between the two rows. This is convincingly brought out by having this imperforate condition featured in a pair.

Other Errors

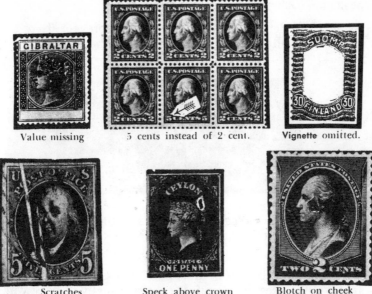

Value missing   5 cents instead of 2 cent.   Vignette omitted.

Scratches   Speck above crown   Blotch on cheek

Flaw

May be a speck or blemish, small blotch, blurr or scratch or crease which occurred during manufacture of paper or printing. May also be due to unclean printing or clogged ink or cracked plates. Flaws are not recognized as true errors. Increases in value due to these finds are usually a matter of opinion and controversy.

Printed over fold.   Foreign matter off.   Printed over fold

Freaks

These are due to accidents during the process of printing stamps. Sometimes a corner of a sheet is unintentionally turned over during the printing. Part of the design will be printed on the normal sheet and the other part on the turned over corner. Other errors classified as freaks are where some foreign substance appears by accident on the printing surface during press operation. When the foreign matter falls off after the printing its shape shows up as a blank space on the stamp.

CANCELLATIONS AND POSTMARKS

Cancellation (Obliterator)

A means of defacing a stamp in order to prevent its re-use. These are usually divided into two parts, the killer and the postmark.

Postmark

That portion of the cancellation of a stamp that gives date, the name of post office, time, etc.

Killer

This is a cancellation or that part of a cancellation which actually obliterates the stamp. It consists usually of bars, wavy lines, etc.

Cancelled to Order

Issues usually cancelled in full sheets by governments but not having served any postal duty. The purpose is to enable these stamps to be sold at reduced prices to stamp dealers and collectors. They are therefore obtainable in full sheets with gum and inherit the condition of a new stamp, except having the cancellation. Among the countries having released such stamps to an important extent are Liberia, Nyassa, North Borneo, Labuan, Costa Rica, Montenegro, Russia, Jugoslavia, Hungary, Bulgaria, etc.

Colored Cancellations

These refer to those colors used outside of the regular black cancellations. These may be due to error as well as being ordinary. In most instances these command a premium over the regular black cancellations. If possible these should be retained on the entire cover.

Cancelled by Favor

Stamps cancelled by the post office to oblige a purchaser. This may have an ordinary or special cancellation. It is often the practice of the post office to return the cancelled mail matter to the sender, even though it has not served any postal duty. This service is usually availed of on occasions by collectors and dealers of first day covers.

Bar Cancellation

This refers particularly to a cancellation used for the express purpose of closing out remainders and enabling the stamps to be sold at greatly reduced prices under face value. Cancellations are usually in the form of parallel bars or lines. See Costa Rica 1901-3 Issues. Labuan, North Borneo, etc.

Cork Cancellations

Generally found on early issues. Cancellations impressed by cork or wood hand-stamp device. Some Postal Clerks cut more or less artistic designs like stars, etc. into the cork or wood used for cancelling stamps. Some of these cancellations are prized and command premiums. Also valued according to the color of the cancellation. Listed in Scott's Specialized U. S. Catalog.

Cut Cancellation

Incisions, or slits cut into stamps as a means of cancellation.
The most common example of these are to be found in the
U. S. Revenue Issues of 1898-1914.

Fiscal (Revenue) Cancellations

From a philatelic viewpoint, the only significance of these
cancellations is to distinguish revenue stamps used for postal
duty from those used solely for revenue purposes. The fiscal
cancellations are usually by penmark or in form of numerals,
spheres, etc. "Tollur" by Iceland, is an example. Also cancelled
by large violet ellipses. However, not all these aforementioned
cancellations are necessarily fiscal. Pen cancellations were
widely used on postal matter before the cancellation machine
was invented. Exceptions such as the use of fiscal cancellations for postal purposes are acceptable only if supported by
covers or other proof.

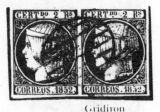

Gridiron

Handstamped

Gridiron Cancellation

A common form of cancellation especially used on early
Stamps. Consists of parallel lines in the shape of a gridiron
which may or may not be within a circle.

Hand-Stamped Cancellations and Postmarks

Applied by hand. This was generally practiced before the
cancellation machine era.

Hole Cancellations

Cancellations punched in stamps such as holes to denote use.

Last Day Cancellation

This shows the last day and location of a discontinued post office. This may be brought on by transfer, change of name or termination.

Meter Mail (Self Cancelling)

Through means of an automatic machine, impressions of prepaid postmarks are made on mail matter. Such mail matter is accepted as precancelled by the post office. Perforated gummed strips are also supplied for parcel post and other bulky matter. While in use the machine simultaneously registers the amount of postage used up. Additional postage can be procured by payment and adjustment of the meter at the post office. It is to be especially pointed out that this type of mail does not involve any adhesive stamps. It represents a permit with sanction of government to make private prepaid postmarks in place of stamps.

Back Stamp

A postmark stamped on the backs of a cover bearing date of arrival, receiving office, etc. In modern times these are applied mostly on registered and special delivery mail.

Paid Cancellation

Often hand-stamped on early U. S. mail matter and postage stamps to indicate prepayment of postage by sender. After 1856 the utlization of regular U.S. stamps fully implied the prepayment of postage and therefore no further need for "Paid" cancellations over mail matter.

Paquebot (Mail Boat) Cancellations

This applies to mail posted on board ship. Upon arrival it is handed to postal authorities at the post office and is usually cancelled with a special "Paquebot" stamp.

Ship Cancellations

A distinctive cancellation made in the post office of a ship. Usually bears name of the ship.

Railroad Cancellations

Applied by a railroad either on the train, at terminal, or at the railroad post office.

Pen Cancellations (Manuscript)

Those used for postal purposes are found mostly in the earlier emissions when some of the post offices were not yet equipped with obliterating devices. Pen cancellations are also known to have been utilized as a means of obliterating revenue stamps.

Advertisement or Slogan Cancellations

Adjacent to or part of a cancellation. Utilized for announcements of communal or national interest such as patriotic propaganda, conservation, postal advice and services, resorts, fund raising events, etc. Also for promoting products and interests of a private nature.

LUMINESCENCE

Luminescence applies to stamps, postal stationery or postal cards produced with a special luminescent ink or given a phosphor coating for the purpose of speeding up the sorting and cancelling of mail. This condition is not noticeable to the eye. Through the use of an ultraviolet detecting device the coating is made recognizable by means of a glow. In U. S. stamps a greenish glow indicates regular postal stamps; a reddish glow indicates airmail stamps. As part of an electronic process these will be automatically faced, separated as well as cancelled.

PHOSPHOR TAGGED

Phospor Tagged: Stamps on which has been applied a phosphorescent coating (see Luminescence)

PRECANCELS

Refers particularly to United States precanceled stamps. These are usually recognized by the name of a town and state overprinted on them. Such overprints serve as a cancellation prior to use. Time is saved as there is no need for cancelling by the post office mail matter bearing such stamps. Other countries issuing precancelled stamps are Belgium, Canada, France and Luxembourg.

Bureau Prints (Precancels)

Applies to stamps which are precancelled by the U. S. Bureau of Engraving and Printing during the printing process and are thus completed before being sent to the towns where they are to be used.

Local Precancels

Stamps cancelled in advance by a local post office prior to sale to the public. This is in order to save time in handling. These stamps are known as local precancels and are distinguished from Bureau Prints issued by the U. S. Bureau of Engraving and Printing in Washington, D. C.

Foreign precancels

Marginal Controls

This applies to certain plate numbers, letters or markings found on sheet margins. These indicate the plate or cylinder from which the sheet was printed. Also may be a means of identifying the year and source of printing, date, and series of issue. They are sometimes helpful for accounting purposes.

Corner Letters

Observed on early English issues. These were for control or checking purposes.

Controls (Underprinted)

These controls are printed on the back of stamps. They may be in the form of a posthorn, as in the case of Sweden 1886-91 Issues and Star for New Zealand 1925. Spain, to check stock of various districts, had blue control numbers on the back of most of its stamps from 1900 to 1932, and Brazil from 1941 to 1944.

Control Marks (Official Control Overprints)

A means of controlling the distribution of certain missing stocks of stamps in order to trace or prevent their use. This may have been necessitated by pilferage, insurrection, stock disappearance, etc. For example, use of certain marks or overprints on remaining stocks of stamps would invalidate and make useless those lacking the overprint.

Initialed (Perforated) Stamps

Initials of business firms sometimes are punched over the face of stamps. This is to avoid, or to assist in tracing the theft of postage stamps by employees. However, perforated initials have another purpose. For instance, Australia perforates O.S. on stamps which means "Official Service."

Private Controls

Utilized by private interests to check stock and to safeguard it against theft. For instance, Ceylon stamps are found with the private name "CAVE" printed over them. This was to prevent use on the outside. Initialed perforated stamps may also be included in this category.

the 24c carmine rose and blue Inverted Plane (Scott C3a) was sold on May 29, 1974 for the record price of $47,000 at the H.R. Harmer, Inc. sale. (also see page 137)

The 30c blue and carmine of the 1869 Issue with Flags inverted is almost perfectly centered, and the colors are rich and distinct. This stamp sold for $32,000.

POSTAL STATIONERY (ENTIRES)

Comprises envelopes, postal cards, airmail and postal letter sheets, newspaper wrappers and other wrappers, etc., which have a stamp printed or embossed thereon.

VARIOUS COVERS AND CHARACTERISTICS

Entires

Applies to envelopes, Government postal cards, various letter sheets and other postal stationery in their entire state, including stamps, after they have served postal duty.

Covers

Refers to entire envelopes which have served postal duty.

First Day Cover.
Cachet handstamped on right

First Flight Cover

First Day Cover

A cover which went through the mails bearing stamps the first day issued. This is supported by a postmark bearing the actual date and also usually by a special cachet stamped on the envelope in celebration of the occasion.

Cachet

A commemorative design usually rubber-stamped or printed on envelopes. This is in celebration of some event and will generally state the date and importance of the occasion. Generally used on the first day of the event. May be either of official or private origin.

First Flight Covers

Covers that have been carried in the first flight over a new air route. They usually bear a dated cancellation to substantiate the occasion.

Envelopes

Refers to entire envelopes intended for postal duty with printed stamp. May be for postal, airmail or official use. Includes those with attached stamps.

Early Stampless Cover   Letter Sheet Folded

Stampless Covers

Refers to covers or folded letters used prior to the adhesive stamp era. Nevertheless they usually bear postmarks or other postal stampings, such as "mailed collect," "postage prepaid," etc.

Letter Sheets

A sheet of paper which, after a message is written on the inside, can be folded and sealed into the form of an envelope. The address is written on the outside which bears a government printed stamp thereon. Should be distinguished from stampless covers, which were used before the emergence of the postage stamp. In modern times letter sheets are available from post offices of many countries.

Air Letter Sheets

Same as the letter sheet, but used exclusively for air post. There will naturally be an airmail stamp printed on the address side.

Wrappers

Procured in sheet form. Of extra length so that they can be used to wrap newspapers and magazines. Usually gummed at one end and bearing an embossed or printed stamp.

Patriotic Covers

These apply particularly to the Civil War era. Used both in the Union and the Confederacy. Characterized by patriotic designs, illustrations, caricatures, slogans, etc. Sought after by historical societies and museums as well as by collectors. Caution should be exercised in their purchase. By means of a loose stamp and an appropriate but unrelated envelope, a forgery of an apparently used patriotic cover may be manufactured by a dishonest source.

Valentine Covers

More in vogue among the earlier issues. These are usually very decorative as well as appropriate for the occasion. This applies as well to the enclosures. Envelopes postmarked on Valentine's Day are preferred.

Zeppelins (or Zep Covers)

Refers to the covers as well as cards carried on flights by the famous German dirigibles as the Graf Zeppelin, the Von Hindenburg, etc.

Crash (or Wreck) Covers

These have been recovered from plane crashes, shipwrecks or other accidents. They are expected to show some sign of the disaster as being partially burnt or water soaked. Where convincing signs are lacking an explanatory label or cachet is affixed to the cover.

Postal Cards

These are convenient medium size cards available to the public for short messages. The front side bears the government stamp and is reserved for the name and address. The other side is for the message by the sender.

Reply Postcard

Has two cards usually perforated or folded between. One of these is for the message and the other for the reply.

| Cut Square | Cut to shape | Tied to cover |

Cut Square

This is the printed stamp on envelopes, wrappers, airmail and letter sheets, postal cards and other postal stationery which has been cut off in square or rectangular shape with ample margin all around. This has been found to be more convenient than attempting to collect full size envelopes.

Cut To Shape

Refers to stamps, especially from envelopes which have been cut to the shape of the design instead of a square or rectangular with adequate margins. Cutting to shape depreciates their desirability and value.

Albinos

Embossed impressions of stamps such as have been observed on envelopes but colorless. This happens during manufacture when by accident, two envelope sheets are fed into the press together. The top sheet receives the full impression but the one underneath receives only the impress of the embossing die without color. This creates an albino variety. The presence of any of these among normal stock is usually due to escape from inspection. They are nevertheless valid for postage.

Tied To Cover

An entire cover with part of the cancellation on the stamp and the other part extended over to the cover.

CONDITION

The condition of a stamp is of major importance in any appraisal of its desirability or value. The zenith of condition of any stamp is when it is in its mint state just after sale by the post office and especially when blessed with well balanced centering. However on used stamps it depends on its state of preservation, degree of cancellation, centering, etc. In offering older or better class stamps, it is common practice for auctioneers and dealers to describe their condition as mint, superb, very fine, fine, good, fair, average, poor, bad, damaged. These terms are interpreted in a following chapter.

From the viewpoints of both prestige and investment, it is advisable to have stamps whenever possible, in the very best of condition. A few defective copies of stamps in an otherwise well conditioned collection, may depreciate the value and respect of the entire collection far out of proportion to the actual value of the damaged stamps. Such circumstances are usually noticed and taken advantage of to the utmost by prospective buyers.

In appraising condition, one must take into consideration the circumstances and general standards of the time when the stamp was first issued. It is not to be expected that an 1860 stamp would be in as superb a condition as a modern stamp. From a comparative point of view, stamps over 50 years old or an issue noted for poor centering and perforations should warrant higher respect than stamps recently printed although classified alike in condition. The world's most expensive stamp British Guiana 1856, 1c is both a poor and damaged copy. In spite of that it is worth $280,000. Here is a good example where an appreciation for rarity overcomes the factor of condition.

Before expecting perfection of a stamp much depends upon how many real good copies were originally released. All copies of a particular stamp may have been printed off center. It would then be almost impossible to find any copy in top condition. Any specimen of such an issue even approaching good centering could be accepted as in superb or very fine condition provided the stamp deserves that rating in all other respects. In such an instance, the reputable dealer will explain the circumstances to the customer to justify the high rating in condition and to eliminate the possibility of misunderstanding.

There seem to be unjustified demands and concern over the condition of stamps of the older types. This may be warranted where a stamp was issued in profuse quantities. However, there are many stamps between 75 to 100 years old. To procure some of these scarcer specimens in prime condition are usually outside the reach or budget of the average collector. In such circumstances there is absolutely no reason why any of the scarcer specimens in lesser condition or those which have even defects should be snubbed. Considering diminishing supply and scarcity, even damaged copies may be precious. What material, whether wood, metal or any hard substance can be expected to last so many years without some deterioration? And stamps are only made out of paper.

Unused

Implies that the stamp has not served postal duty. This is regardless of whether or not it is any longer gummed. However, where the original gum is missing this should be mentioned on the back of the stamp, if it is offered as an unused stamp.

VARIOUS DEGREES OF CONDITION

These terms are usually mentioned in the general stamp trade. The following degrees specified pertain to stamps whose original condition were under normal circumstances.

Mint

A stamp so described must be in good condition as when issued. It must be unused with full original gum and without the least defect. Although it may not be well centered or have good margins around it, it may still be considered a mint stamp as long as it was so issued. If an unused stamp has no gum it cannot be accepted as mint unless it was originally issued without gum. Unused stamps are sometimes described with the letters o.g., which means that the stamp has the original gum.

SELF GUIDED TOUR—WASHINGTON, D.C.
BUREAU OF ENGRAVING AND PRINTING

All visitors to the nations capitol are welcome to pass through and inspect the various equipment and machinery used in the processing and packaging of postage stamps (as well as currency). On view will be the ultra modern intalio multi-colored printing of commemorative stamps. Other operations connected with the work and materials may also be observed. The main building is located at 14th and "C" Streets, S.W. Visitors enter at the 14th Street entrance. Open to the public each workday Monday to Friday between 8 A.M. to 2:30 P.M. The tour is free of charge and usually takes about 25 minutes. Accessible by bus. Also within walking distance of the downtown hotels and shopping area.

Superb

Of extraordinary all-around condition with appearance like a new stamp, well balanced centering, clean and unsoiled, without the slightest defect or injury to the body of the stamp. Unused stamps so classified should possess the original gum unless issued without gum. Used stamps should be clearly but lightly cancelled. Imperforates should have ample margins around.

Very Fine

Conspicuous as a stamp in prime and clean condition. May be well centered but not necessarily to the degree of mathematical perfection. All its perforations must be intact and have full original gum (if issued with such) and be entirely free from the slightest flaw or defect.

Fine

Outstanding in condition over average stamp. May not have perfect centering or have the freshness of a superb or very fine copy but there should be no defect or damage to the body or design of the stamp. Hinge marks are permissible but not to the degree of a thin spot. None of the perforations should be missing although a few may be slightly short. The postmark should not be too heavy. Unused stamps should still possess the original gum if so issued.

Good (or Fair)

May be off center (not extreme), heavily cancelled (not big blotch) have hinge mark (but not thin spot), have some perforations short, have crease (not severe), be straight edged but otherwise no bodily defect or damage.

Average

Representative of the average condition of stamps to be found among the lower grades of quality, but with no bodily defect or damage.

Poor

May be heavily cancelled, badly centered, have a tear, thin spot, crease, missing perforations, etc., but to a moderate extent and degree.

Bad

Stamps should be so described if they have extreme faults such as heavily cancelled (very large or a big bloth) deep tear, holes, skinned paper, several perforations missing, severe creases, or a faded or discolored surface.

Cut Close

Refers to imperforate stamps that have been trimmed or cut too close to the design.

Cut Into

Stamps which have had their design cut into by perforating or cutting machines during the process of separation.

Seconds

This is a lot which most collectors or dealers accumulate. Made up of stamps of unacceptable or inferior quality. Into this pile are usually thrown defective stamps of the slightest to the most extreme degree depending upon the whims or opinions of the accumulator. These are usually disposed of at very liberal price reductions or as a bargain lot.

As Is

This is a term sometimes used in describing a lot for which the purchaser bears the responsibility as to the count, condition, character and quality.

Damaged

Any kind of injury to the body of a stamp no matter how slight or on what part. Among the most common of these are tears, thin spots and the loss of one or more perforations. Although not desirable, heavily cancelled stamps, those not well centered, or with straight edges are not considered as damaged stamps. With this topic it is also advisable to read the chapter on hinges. In the offering of any damaged stamp, its condition should be marked on the back.

Expertizing

To have a stamp examined and certified by an authority or a board of experts. Some philatelic organizations such as the American Philatelic Society have a special committee for this purpose.

Heavily Cancelled Stamps

These are less desirable and valued than those with lighter cancellations. Therefore heavily cancelled stamps should be avoided or replaced if possible by the lighter types.

Repaired Stamps

This art is usually confined to the more expensive and worthwhile specimens. In view of the vast difference in value between good and damaged specimens of some stamps, the intent of the dealer in the handling of damaged stamps is of some concern. Although there is nothing wrong in the repair or ownership of such a stamp, it is a fraud if sold as an undamaged or faultless stamp. The damaged condition of any stamp should always be so mentioned by any honest dealer (usually noted on the back). Repairs will be usually revealed by putting the stamp in Benzine or have it broken apart by soaking it in water.

Skinned (or Thinned)

This is when part of the paper of a stamp has been stripped or pulled apart. The most common cause is its careless and forceful removal from an envelope without utlizing one of the safer methods such as soaking it off in water. See also Thin Spot.

Straight Edged

Some Sheets (or panes) have perforations on all sides of its stamps except those on its edges which are cut straight. Therefore stamps which border on these edges have one or more straight edges. Although such varieties are not considered as defective, and are comparatively scarcer than the fully perforated stamps, they do not command as high respect and prices as the normal types with perforations all around. However, coil stamps which have either horizontal or vertical normal straight sides are not classified as straight edged.

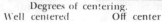
Degrees of centering.

Perfect   Well centered   Off center   Badly centered

Centering

This refers to the degree of perfection (or equality) of the margins around the central printed design of a stamp. Stamps are described as well centered when the margins are of well distance all around. Those noticeably not well balanced are considered off center. In an extreme case of bad centering the perforations may pass through the actual printed design. In the case of imperforated stamps, bad centering may result in one or more of the margins being cut away or cut into the design.

Crease   Thin Spot

Crease (or Fold)

Considered an imperfection in a stamp if it cannot be removed. To lessen or possibly remove a crease, soak the stamp in water for a few minutes. While still damp, place it face downward on a hard surface. Cover it with a piece of paper and carefully press a hot iron over the creased area. Or after soaking you may be able to remove the crease by rubbing that part of the stamp with your thumb nail. Then put the stamp under a heavy weight. However caution should be exercised on surface coated stamps or those with fugitive inks.

Thin Spot

This is a thinning of the paper, usually visible on the back of a stamp, which has been caused by the careless or forceable removal of a hinge. Most often it is the result of using hinges which are not peelable or are otherwise unsuitable. It can also be due to using too much moisture and causing an overflow of water. CAUTION: Be sure not to remove a hinge until it is absolutely dry.

REPRINTS, SPURIOUS AND CONTROVERSIAL ISSUES

The detection of questionable issues is one of the chief and necessary tasks of the true student of philately. To some this comes instinctively or by experience. Some collectors handling rarities go to the extent of having a well-equipped laboratory, with chemicals, measuring instruments and a quarz lamp using ultra-violet rays to analyze materials and do other detective work to expose forgeries and fakes. We must thank these devoted sons of philately, the stamp periodicals and the collectors' societies, for constantly exposing these spurious issues and thus helping to keep the hobby clean. Some collectors have a so-called rogues' gallery collection. Any time they get one of these worthless specimens they add it to this collection for comparative purposes. However, wide distribution of these is not to be encouraged. Questionable stamps should be directed for attention and study to well-intentioned collectors or to stamp societies like the American Philatelic Society, American Stamp Dealers Association, etc. Most stamp societies have expertizing committees.

Stamps known to have been reprinted.

Reprints

These represent stamps which have been reprinted from old plates of discontinued stamps for sale to collectors. They are not valid for postage. This may be a direct act of the government or of speculators with the permission of the government. Even though they are printed from original plates, reprints are usually detected as it is very difficult to match exactly the paper, color, gum, etc., of the original stamps. However, do not mistake reprints for facsimiles, counterfeits and forgeries. Whereas reprints are printed with the original plates, the others are pure imitations made from new plates.

Typical Seebeck reprints

Seebeck Reprints

The impact that these issues have made on the stamp collecting world has been so deep, that the name Seebeck in philately is almost synonymous with the term reprint. Applies particularly to certain Latin American Stamps named after Nicholas F. Seebeck who was associated with the Hamilton Bank Note Company. Between 1890 and 1899 he contracted to supply each year a new set of stamps to Ecuador, Honduras, Nicaragua and Salvador. No charge was made for these stamps but it was agreed that all unsold stamps of a replaced issue were to be made invalid for postage and returned to Seebeck. He also had the right to use the original plates to make reprints. The compensation Seebeck derived was from the sales of such stamps to collectors and dealers at a fraction of the face value.

Typical Seebeck reprints

The Seebeck reprints can be identified by the thick porous paper on which they were printed, whereas the originals are on a thinner and stiffer stock. An original specimen is much more prized when it is on an actual used cover. Although many years have elapsed since they were issued, the status and importance of these Seebeck reprints are still controversial. However, there is no doubt that the attractiveness of these stamps and their enterprising promotion did much to draw many new recruits into the field of philately.

Spurious Issues

This applies to those stamps which were deliberately manufactured or changed for the purpose of defrauding the stamp collector. Among these may be included counterfeits or forgeries.

Some typical counterfeits of stamps

Counterfeits (Forgeries)

Of entirely private issue for the sole purpose of imitating stamps to defraud the government or stamp collector. However, where the fraud is directed against collectors the scope may extend to the imitation of overprints and surcharges. Naturally these would be confined to the more expensive varieties. Counterfeits and forgeries were more common in the early days of philately. In former times, stamp collecting was not so well organized as today, when questionable material is exposed by the philatelic press, stamp societies and other agencies. Therefore old collections particularly should be scrutinized for counterfeits and forgeries. No matter how skillful or perfect a forgery there will be some difference in the printing, color, paper, gum, perforations, etc. which the experienced philatelist will be able to notice. It is fortunate that most spurious specimens are thus detected.

Fake

A stamp that has been altered, changed or treated so as to represent a more valuable variety. This may be accomplished by altering or cutting away perforations in order to pass the specimen off as part perforated. Also colors may be changed by exposure or the use of chemicals; and grills and cancellations may be removed or repairs made with intent to defraud.

Some facsimiles of stamps.

Facsimiles

An outright imitation of a stamp, and so represented without intent to defraud. However, material of this nature should be honestly described when offered.

Bogus Stamps

Stamps which have not been issued by a recognized or existent government. Most are of private origin, especially for disposal to collectors. This kind of material is not to be classified as stamps. They are in the category of labels and philatelically are seldom worth more than the paper on which they are printed. Examples are Bolivian Railway Issue, and some unauthorized Confederate Stamps.

Poster Stamps

The only distinction that these have from being considered just ordinary labels are that they usually come in long series such as Presidents of the United States, Animals of the World, Adventures of Marco Polo, etc. They are usually put up in booklet form or by sheet with a special album for their use.

Private Issues

These are divided into two classes. Those with the sanction of the government such as local issues and the U. S. 1864-1899 Match and Medicine Revenue Stamps. In this category may also be included Telegraph, Aviation, Welfare and other stamps serving private interests. In the other group are those which have been privately made as labels, poster stamps, and facsimiles designed to imitate or resemble regular stamps.

INDIA

Labels

These are distinguished according to the intent. If the purpose is to masquerade as or to resemble stamps they could be classified as Bogus Stamps (see latter). On the other hand they could belong to the large family of legitimate labels which may include such subjects of philatelic interest as flags of the world, coats of arms, etc. The latter group is very popular and well received by juvenile collectors for decorative purposes in albums.

Seals

form of label especially utilized as a seal or a decoration on an envelope. Philatelically the best known of these are the annual Christmas Seals listed by Scott's U. S. Specialized Catalog. Seals are issued by various philatelic societies and exhibitions for advertising and promoting philatelic events sponsored by them. There is also a government seal used by the post office to seal and repair mail matter. See Post Office Seals.

STAMPS SOLICITED FOR REHABILITATION

For more than 60 years the Graymoor Friars (Stamp Department) Garrison, N. Y. 10524, have been operating the St. Christopher Inn as a refuge for Alcoholics and broken down physical men. As part of the treatment these men are given light work as washing and assorting stamps. This has proven to have great therapeutic value in assisting unfortunates to regain confidence and health and be put back in society as useful citizens. Contributions of any kind of stamps are needed in order to continue this highly commendable work. Send contributions to Graymoor Stamp Department, Graymoor, Garrison, N. Y. 10524.

Speculative Issues

These are stamps whose object is more for sale to stamp collectors than to serve postal duty. There is no doubt that the number of stamps issued by pint-sized countries like San Marino, Monaco, Andorra and Liechtenstein, go far beyond their postal needs. However, courting the collector's dollar is not limited to just midget countries. Russia, Hungary, Czechoslovakia, Belgium and Romania are also more or less hungry for this business.

Chemically Cleaned

Stamps from which the cancellations have been chemically removed. This constitutes fraud if utilized in the removal of cancellations from used stamps with the object of offering as unused specimens or to using again postally.

Album Weeds

A term utilized to describe stamps of spurious origin as fakes, counterfeits, forgeries, bogus stamps, fascimiles, speculative reprints and others of questionable nature. These should be removed from a stamp album just as the gardener would remove weeds and other undesirable plants from the ground.

Album weeds

The above resemble the genuine stamps but are counterfeits.

LIST OF DON'TS

Don't paste stamps flat in album.

Don't use glue or paste for affixing stamps in album.

Don't use ordinary gummed paper or gummed parts of envelopes for hinges.

Don't remove a wet hinge from a stamp. Wait until it is perfectly dry.

Don't use too much moisture in hinging stamps. The overflow may cause the stamp to stick flat on its back.

Don't remove rare stamps from envelopes or other wrappers. These may be worth much more on cover. Furthermore, removals of rare stamps from covers should be handled only by a skilled collector.

Do not remove plate numbers, or plate names, etc. from blocks of four. These usually add to the value.

Don't remove gum from unused stamps.

Don't handle stamps with unclean hands. The use of stamp tongs will avoid this.

Avoid smudges, creases and tears. These greatly depreciate the value of stamps.

Avoid thin spots by using only peelable hinges. Another way to safeguard against this, especially with more expensive stamps, is to use transparent (hingeless) mounts.

Don't expose stamps to the sunlight by display for any sustained period. This may discolor stamps or remove colors entirely.

Don't let water or other fluids contact chalky or other surface-coated paper, or stamps that have soluble printing inks. This may result in the removal of the design of the ink.

Don't use benzine on stamps printed by photogravure. This removes the ink.

Don't accept stamps of questionable origin or encourage their circulation. This includes such material as counterfeits, forgeries, bogus stamps, facsimiles (so called album weeds) or other material sold with intent to deceive. The better element of philately is always fighting to keep the hobby clean. If these efforts are relaxed the hobby will be eventually flooded with all kinds of worthless labels as well as imitations.

Don't keep your album or any kind of unused stamps near a damp, humid place or expose to excessive heat. This may cause them to stick together or adhere to other matter. Use glassine interleaving between stamps where possible.

Scott's Standard Catalogs

Published in the United States. A widely used reference book. Gives description and value of most all major postage stamps issued in the world to date. In three volumes. There is also available Scott's Specialized U. S. Catalog for specialists in U. S. stamps.

Scott's U. S. Specialized Catalog

Due to the very wide range of U. S. postage, revenues, private and other issues, not all of these are listed in Scott's regular Standard Catalog. It is therefore essential for serious collectors of U. S. stamps to equip themselves with a copy of Scott's U. S. Specialized Catalog. Although omitted in the regular catalog, the following issues are listed in the Specialized Catalog: Postmaster's Provisionals, First Day Covers, Vending Machine Perforations, Booklet Panes, Post Office Seals, Postal Cards, Proofs, Motor Vehicle Stamps, Trial Color Proofs, Specimens, Encased stamps, Locals, Hand-stamped Covers, Telegraphs, Christmas Seals, Playing Cards, Match and Medicine Stamps, Cordial and Wine stamps,

Maynard Sundman   Theodore E. Steinway Patron.

LITTLETON STAMP CO., LITTLETON, N. H.
See page 124

This firm in the approval stamp business, towers over most all the others in the same field. It is the outcome of the tireless energy and enterprise of its founder, Maynard Sundman. After discharge from the army in World War II, with little else to start with than determination and an innate intelligence, he has built up an enormous business to such a dimension that the firm has become one of the leading industries of the fair sized town in which it is located. There are few towns or hamlets where there are no customers to be found of this extensive organization.

U.S. POSTAL SERVICE IN STAMP BUSINESS

As a means of procuring additional revenue, the U.S. Postal Service is now earnestly promoting the sale of stamps, beginners kits, supplies, philatelic publications and other kindred items through many of its post offices.

Antonio Ricaurte
y Lozano
A117

Coat of
Arms
A118

A123

1917   Engraved.

Perf. 14, 11½ and Compound.

339	A107	½c bistre	3	2
340	A108	1c green	4	2
341	A109	2c carmine rose	6	2
342	A110	4c violet	15	8
343	A111	5c dull blue	15	3
344	A112	10c gray	25	3
345	A113	20c red	50	8
346	A114	50c carmine	75	8
347	A115	1p bright blue	1.50	30
348	A116	2p orange	3.00	65
349	A117	5p gray	8.00	2.00
350	A118	10p dark brown	17.50	6.00

The lithographed varieties of Nos. 343, 345 and 346 are now known to be counterfeits made to defraud the government.

1920-21   Lithographed.

Perf. 10, 13½ and Compound.

360	A121	½c yellow	50	15
		a. ½c orange		
361	"	1c green	12	5
362	"	2c red	6	3
		b. Horizontal pair, imperf. between		
363	A122	3c green	8	3
		*a.*3c yellow green	8	3
		*b.*3c bright green	8	3
		c. Printed on both sides		
		d. Horizontal pair, imperf. between		
364	A121	5c blue	15	6
		a. Horizontal pair, imperf. between		
365	"	10c violet	50	15
366	"	20c deep green	2.50	40

1924
379   A124
381   "

1925   Bla

Imp

382   A12
383   A12

Imprint

Part page from Scott's Catalog showing catalog numbers.
Also the unused and used values of each item.

Catalog Numbers

This refers to specific numbers assigned to each variety in Scott's and other standard catalogs. They play an important as well as a convenient role in identifying stamps. An individual price list or an advertisement for instance need only mention the country and Scott's catalog numbers of certain stamps. The prospective purchaser can then look up the numbers referred to in the catalog and usually be able to find the pedigree, description as well as the estimated value of each individual stamp. Also perhaps, supplementary or precautionary notes as well.

Catalog Values

In philately this is generally interpreted as the values for stamps in acceptable condition quoted in catalogs such as Scott's in U. S., Gibbons in England, Yvert in France, Zumstein in Switzerland, etc. In almost every instance dual values are quoted, one for the used and another for unused specimens. It must be realized that these catalogs are of private origin and not of an official nature. Therefore it rests largely upon the opinions of the publishers as to the correct valuations. To maintain accurate and up-to-date market values for an estimated more than 250,000 different major and minor varieties of stamps issued to date, is admittedly an impossible task and therefore catalog values are vulnerable to constant criticism and controversies.

STAMPS AS THERAPY
By Herman Herst, Jr.

Philatelists are justly proud of the program which a number of unselfish individuals have set up to bring the pleasures of the hobby to the less fortunate. Literally hundreds of collectors and dealers work on this on a local scale by contributing and distributing stamps, albums and accessories in children's homes, Veterans' Hospitals, Senior Citizen groups and even penitentiaries.

On a national scale, the work of two men stands out: Ernest A. Kehr, whose Stamps for the Wounded, founded during World War II, brought philately to tens of thousands of hospitalized soldiers, and George Silberberg, whose Hobbies for the Handicapped is sponsored by the charitable New York organization, the Grand Street Boys.

Both organizations receive contributions from collectors and dealers, and process them for distribution to the ultimate reciepients.

Red Cross workers are enthusiastic about stamps in hospitals in which they do volunteer service. Any hobby serves as therapy in such cases, but philately has proven to be an outstanding diversion for giving the sick and wounded a new outlook on life, and to let them know that the outside world has not forgotten them. In penitentiaries particularly, where a progressive policy permits a program of rehabilitation, rather than punishment, stamps have done their part. (At the Ohio State Prison riots in Columbus, at the height of the fire and destruction, the stamp club President asked the Warden to permit a meeting of his group, to show that not one of the members was participating in demonstrations which ended in the loss of so many lives. Not one member failed to show up.)

Individuals who have returned to normal life after spending a period of time in hospitals or prisons have taken their philatelic pursuits with them. Many remained collectors the rest of their lives; several entered the stamp trade.

"Hobbies for the Handicapped" may be contacted through George I. Silberberg, Grand Street Boys, 2122 Wallace Avenue, Bronx, New York 10462, while "Stamps for the Wounded" may be reached through Ernest A. Kehr, 220 West 42nd Street, New York 10036.

Catalog Illustrations

As a means of identification the catalog refers to an illustration therein of a stamp with a design (or frame) distinct from any other and assigns it a key number. Although stamps may differ in denominations, color, etc., they are considered of the same key if the general pattern of the design is the same or typical of the key stamp illustrated.

Government Publication on U. S. Stamps

Entitled Postage Stamps of the United States. Covers all stamps issued from 1847 to time book went to press. Fully illustrated. Write to U. S. Government Printing Office, Washington 25, D. C.

STAMP MIXTURES

Stamps so described represent mixed lots of stamps on or off paper or both. They are expected to contain duplicates, which frequently are found to a large extent. There are various kinds of mixtures such as Ordinary, Mission, Bank (Commercial House), Cuttings, Kiloware, Government sealed, Revenue, Letter-mail, Waste Paper, etc. depending upon the source of the accumulation. Mixtures may be described also as picked or unpicked. The unpicked naturally command a higher price. Mixture described as unpicked, indicates that nothing has been removed from the original contents.

Ordinary Grade Mixture

This denotes the regular common grade confined almost entirely to low postal denominations. Also there may be a more or less of a sprinkling of commemoratives, airpost, special deliveries, etc. This is just the kind of letter mail mixture that would be accumulated by an average domestic firm. Only the corner of the envelope or wrapper on which the stamps are affixed is withheld as part of the mixture. The other part of the cover is thrown away as waste. This grade is usually abundant on the market and sold by the weight.

Mission mixture in package form

Mission Mixture

As its name implies, the source is usually missions and churches. By habit this term has been adopted also to apply to mixtures from hospitals and other welfare institutions gathered and donated by members or the public for fund raising purposes. As this kind of mixture is usually made up of the more common grade it is frequently sold in large accumulations.

Bank Mixture

Although by name it is assumed to be from a bank, the term is used technically to describe a mixture of high quality such as would be required for heavy postage, air mail and important matter. Among the best sources of this material, besides financial institutions are large commercial houses, exporters, importers and any other firms engaged in foreign trade. Usually sold on paper by weight or as accumulated at a high premium. One must not assume the erroneous impression that any stamp mixture from a bank is of high quality just because it comes from a bank. Some stamp mixtures from banks are just as common as any ordinary letter mail mixture, especially those from banks engaged only in local or domestic trade. Yes, a bank mixture technically is supposed to be of very good quality but before purchase it is sound policy to make sure that the contents live up to expectations.

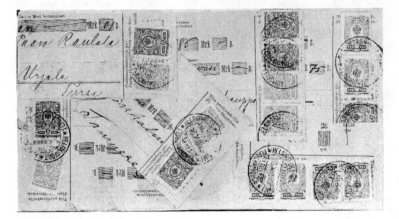

Cuttings

A mixture in which the stamps are attached to part of the cards originally used for money orders, dispatch documents, receipts, parcel post, etc. Due to the heavy weight of the card waste, the number of stamps to the pound is far below that of ordinary letter mail.

111

The Collectors Club, Inc.

Host to Philately

This is a very commendable society dedicated to the advancement, preservation and dispensing of philatelic knowledge. It occupies its own building of classical beauty and charm. The structure was originally built as a millionaire's private residence. It was designed by the ever famous architect, Sanford White. The club was founded in 1896. Among its charter members were the legendary patriarchs of philately, John N. Luff and John W. Scott. It has five floors. At the entrance is its artistic plate glass door mounted in wrought iron. After passing through you enter a majestic foyer of white marble with ornate Grecian columns. At the left wall it has a homelike fireplace. Among the elegant furnishings are paintings, recessed alcoves and decorative art objects. Good fellowship and clubby atmosphere is reflected in the warmth of its comfortable lounge

When sunshine prevails, rays of cheerfulness pour through its wide palatial bay window. Scattered throughout the floors are meeting, study, exhibit, lecture, administrative and conference rooms. All these facilities are not only for the club members but available also for other philatelic organizations. Among these are Masonic Stamp Club, The Czecho Philatelic Society, Judaica Historica Society, Hellenic Philatelic Society, etc. The club has regular scheduled meetings and a printed program of lectures for the season. Its philatelic library which is by far the foremost in the world has over 140,000 items. These are available to members in accordance with the rules. With the membership is included its scholarly bi-monthly "The Collectors Club Philatelist." The organization lends itself also to outside social and fraternal activities. Frequently there are enjoyable dinners in nearby restaurants in which good humour and friendliness predominates.

NOTE: The Philatelic Library has also been made available to the general public.

For brochure and application blank apply to the Executive Secretary, The Collectors Club, 22 East 35th St., New York, N.Y. 10016. Dues are $50.00 per year for resident members; $15.00 annually for non-resident members.

Mixture on Paper

This mixture is made up only of the corners or those parts of the envelopes, wrappers, etc. that hold the stamps. The other parts of the coverings are discarded as waste paper. This kind of material is usually sold by the weight. In buying such mixture it is important to have an estimate of the number of stamps per lb. as the figure may be as high as 3,500; or to as little as only a few hundred where the stamps are on heavy wrapping paper, cards or carton cuttings.

Government Sealed Mixtures

These are packaged and sealed under the supervision of various governments, such as Denmark, Norway, Sweden, Finland, Hungary, Czechoslovakia, Jugoslavia, etc. Put up usually in one kilo boxes (2.20 lbs.). Also dated by the year. The price depends sometimes on the period covered. These mixtures are supposedly of unpicked material and because they are thus sealed, carry reasonable assurance against tampering. Sold usually at a premium.

Kiloware

This is the technical name for stamp mixtures on paper and as its name implies it is offered by the weight or kilo. A kilo is equal to 2.20 pounds. This is the customary term of most foreign sources for transactions involving stamp mixtures.

Letter Mail Mixtures

This is descriptive of stamp mixtures derived entirely from ordinary mail as distinct from that derived from catalog, parcel post and other mail with heavy coverings. The chief significance of the term is the assurance that many stamps are to be expected per pound in view of the lightness of the waste matter torn from the envelope which holds the stamps.

Waste Paper Mixture

This describes a mixture usually composed of the common grade where stamps are on the entire envelopes or wrappers or other coverings, just as found in the waste paper basket. This is prior to converting it into a mixture customarily described as mixture on paper.

Mixture Off Paper (Washed Stamps)

When a stamp mixture is described as "off paper" (or "washed") it indicates that stamps have been soaked off paper to which it was attached as envelopes, etc. There may be as many as 10,000 stamps off paper to the pound. This term should not be mistaken for those stamps classified as "cleaned," which customarily means specimens which have been chemically treated to remove cancellations with intent to defraud or for re-use as postage.

U. S. Revenue Mixture

This applies especially to U. S. 1914-56 Documentary, Future Delivery and other revenue stamps on complete documents. Mixed in among same may also be found State Documentary Stamps as well. Usually available after housecleaning on the part of stock exchange houses and disposal of old records. Sometimes obtainable in very large quantity. Since the amount of waste matter is large the price per pound is usually low.

Soaking Stamps Off Paper

The process of removing stamps from the paper to which it is attached. The customary as well as old fashioned method is to soak in water sufficiently until the attached paper peels off easily. Then put the stamps down on an absorbent surface as a blotter. If the stamps coil after being dried they can be pressed down by a weight. CAUTION: Do not soak in liquid any stamps with ink or paper coating that can be dissolved. Also do not use steaming or hot water as this may cause colors to run off. Cold water is the safest to use.

Find

This refers to an exceptional stamp that has been unexpectedly found in an ordinary mixture or lot.

A MOST DISTINGUISHED PHILATELIST

HARRY L. LINDQUIST (PUBLISHER)

For fame, accomplishments and as a philatelic authority, Harry L. Lindquist is probably the most ornamental figure in Stampdom to-day.

He has a long and conspicuous background in the field of philately which dates back to the early 1900's when he was active in the Chicago Philatelic Society and published the renowned Collector's Journal and many other philatelic classics. After serving in the first World War he was connected with several trade publications in Chicago and New York. In 1932 he revived his own publishing firm with his excellent "STAMPS MAGAZINE' and philatelic books as his major interest. "STAMPS MAGAZINE" reflects his high policies and ethics. Its pages are devoid of scandal, sensationalism, prejudice or self-interest.

In 1932 he also founded the National Federation of Stamp Clubs of which he is still president, and has served as judge and commissioner of many International Shows in the U.S. and abroad.

He was elected to the British Roll of Distinguished Philatelists in 1947 and was awarded the Alfred F. Lichtenstein Memorial Award in 1957. He is a Fellow of the Royal Philatelic Society, London, and holds life membership in the Collectors Club of New York, as well as honorary membership in scores of others.

He was a member of the first Citizens' Stamp Advisory Committee, which was inaugurated by Postmaster General Arthur E. Summerfield, and was appointed Chairman of the People-to-People Hobbies Committee by President Eisenhower in 1956 to promote friendship and understanding between Americans and citizens of other lands. Over a million contacts were made with stamp collectors throughout the world through First Day Covers alone.

He is Chairman of the Founders Membership of the Cardinal Spellman Philatelic Museum, Honorary Chairman of the International Exhibitions sponsored by the Association for Stamp Exhibitions, and a Founder Member of the Masonic Stamp Club.

On occasions he has been honorary chairman of the Philatelic Division of the United Jewish Appeal. His great popularity and influence never fails to draw to such meetings a much larger attendance as well as a substantial increase in contributions.

Outside of his philatelic interests he is a director of the Northern Dispensary, N.Y.C. (founded in 1825) and also that of the Leroy Hospital, N.Y.C. He is a past president of the elite New York Athletic Club.

Diploma given by School of Philately, Fla. to graduates on completion of 20 week course on Stamp Collecting.

STAMP COLLECTORS HANDBOOK

USED AS TEXTBOOK IN TEACHING PHILATELY

There is a widespread use of this publication as a textbook throughout the entire realm of Philately. It is with much satisfaction that we report two additional well known Philatelic Groups that make large use of our Handbook in their courses on Philately. We do not know of any better compliments for this book.

Hollywood School of Philately, Hollywood, Florida

Philatelic Society of Cincinnati, P.O. Box 9086, Cincinnati, O. 45209

Stanley Gibbons Ltd. bought this cover bearing two Nova Scotia Shillings in combination with a 3P and a 6P for $22,000 at the Harmer Sale of the Dale-Lichtenstein Collection 18-21 November 1968.

INTERESTING FACTS ABOUT STAMPS

British Guiana
$280,000

Mauritius
$52,500

Sweden (error)
$35,000

British Guiana
$45,000

SOME OF THE MOST VALUABLE STAMPS IN THE WORLD

British Guiana. 1856 1c Magenta. Valued $280,000 Was accidentally discovered by a boy looking over old papers.

Mauritius Error. 1847 1p orange unused. Valued at $52,500 Inscribed by error Post Office instead of Post Paid.

Sweden 1855 Issue. Supposed to be Europe's' rarest stamp. Error in color. 3c orange instead of blue green. Valued at $35,000.

U. S. Postmasters' Provisional 1846 Issue. Alexandria, Va. Valued on cover at over $32,500

Hawaiian Missionary Stamp. Type Set. Issue, 2c blue. Valued at $55,000

Honduras 1925 Airpost. Surcharged 25c on 10c. (The Blue Honduras.) Valued at $30,000.

U. S. Postmasters' Provisional 1846 Issue. Millbury, Mass., 5c bluish. Valued at $45,000.

U. S. Postmasters' Provisional, 1845 New Haven Issue, 5c envelope stamp. Valued at $32,000

Baden 1851 Issue. Error in color. 9k blue green instead of deep rose. Valued at $30,000.

Hawaii $55,000

Baden (error) $30,000

Honduras $30,000

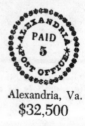
Alexandria, Va.
$32,500

Millbury, Mass. $45,000

New Haven, Conn.
$32,000

LARGEST STAMPS IN THE WORLD

China: World's largest stamp. One of four parts (reduced).
7½ x 2¾ inches. (about 21 square inches)

China; special delivery stamp; 1905-12 Issue; in four parts.
Size 8 x 2½ inches.

China; special delivery stamp; 1913-14 Issue; in four parts.
Size 7½ x 2¾ inches.

United States 1865 Newspaper Stamps. Size 3¾ x 2 inches.

119

SMALLEST STAMPS IN THE WORLD

Colombia: State of Bolivar; Illustration A1 (Scott's), 3 varieties.

Colombia: 1952 Issue, 5c ultramarine. Communications Building.

Victoria 1873-1901, ½p Victoria Midget Size stamps.

Nicaragua 1949 Postal Tax Stamp, 5c blue, National Stadium.

Spain 1872-77, ¼c small crown stamps.

Highest Denomination

Germany 1923 Inflation Issue. 50,000,000,000 Marks.

Highest United States Stamp. 1950 Distilled Spirits $50,000 tax stamp. Scott's No. RX25 (Spec. Catalog).

Number of Collectors in U. S. and World

In the United States there are estimated to be 25,000,000 active and intermittent stamp collectors. In the world there are estimated to be 75,000,000 stamp collectors. It has been established that half of all individuals have saved postage stamps sometime or other during their lifetimes.

ANTI SMUGGLING STAMP

This is a 1966 stamp from Philippines (Scott No. 946) with overprint "HELP MF STOP SMUGGLING. PRES. MARCOS." Used as part of a campaign to stamp out smuggling.

STAMPS AS A BUSINESS CAREER

Just as in any other business, a person with intelligence, ability and initiative has a good chance of success dabbling in stamps. This may be done first on a part-time basis, which if favored with initial success, may develop into a full-time enterprise. Very few stamp firms are known to have gone bankrupt, even in times of depression. Stamps have developed into big business. The volume of business done by some stamp firms easily surpass a million dollars a year.

THE OLDEST POSTAGE STAMPS

| Great Britain 1840 | Zurich (Switz.) 1843 | Brazil 1843 | Geneva (Switz.) 1843 |

| Basle (Switz.) 1845 | United States 1847 | Mauritius 1847 | Bermuda 1848 |

| France 1849 | Belgium 1849 | Bavaria 1849 | New South Wales 1850 | Spain 1850 |

As issued by the various countries. Also date of Issue.

GREAT BRITAIN	May 6, 1840
ZURICH, Canton of (Switzerland)	Mar. 1, 1843
BRAZIL	July 1, 1843
GENEVA, Canton of (Switzerland)	Oct. 1, 1843
BASLE, Canton of (Switzerland)	July 1, 1845
UNITED STATES	July 1, 1847
MAURITIUS	Sept. 2, 1847
BERMUDA	Mar. 1, 1848
FRANCE	Jan. 1, 1849
BELGIUM	July 1, 1849
BAVARIA	Nov. 1, 1849
NEW SOUTH WALES	Jan. 1, 1850
SPAIN	Jan. 1, 1850

FAMOUS STAMP COLLECTORS — PAST AND PRESENT

Franklin D. Roosevelt, Former U. S. President
King George V of England
King George VI of England
King Fuad of Egypt
Colonel Edward H. R. Green, Financier
Count Philippe la Renotiere von Ferrary
Joseph S. Frelinghuysen, Former U. S. Senator
Theodore E. Steinway, Piano Manufacturer
Alfred F. Lichtenstein, Industrialist
Louise Boyd Dale
Alfred H. Caspary, Stock broker
George H. Worthington, Industrialist
John V. P. Heinmuller, Pres. Longines-Wittnauer Watch Co.
Harold L. Ickes, Former Sec'y of the Interior
Rear Admiral Frederic R. Harris, U. S. Navy
Arthur Hind, Manufacturer
T. K. Tapling, British Financier
H. J. Duveen, Art Dealer
J. L. Luff, Famous Stamp Expert and Author
Alastair Bradley Martin, National Court Tennis Champion
Esmond Bradley Martin, Sportsman and Big game hunter
Charles Lathrop Pack, Conservation authority
Colonel E. Albert Aisenstadt, U. S. Army (retired).
Harry L. Lindquist, Author-Publisher
Colonel Hans Lagerlof, Importer
Francis Cardinal Spellman
Adolphe Menjou, Movie Star
Maurice Burrus, French Financier
Glenn Ford, Movie Star
Jerry Wald, Movie Tycoon
Earl of Crawford, Famous Philatelist
H. J. Crocker, Industrialist
Dr. Clarence W. Hennan, Surgeon
Lauritz Melchior, Opera Star
General Mark W. Clark, U. S. Army
Ernst A. Kehr, Radio-Television Editor and Author
Leon Bamberger, R. K. O. Pictures
Baron Rothschild, French Financier
King Carol of Rumania
Baron Mitsui, Japanese Industrialist
Josiah K. Lilly

Count Ferrary   Arthur Hind   Colonel Green

Count Ferrary Collection

Count Philip la Rénotiere von Ferrary was an Austrian citizen. He had two full time clerks just to assist him in assorting and arranging his stamps. His collection was siezed as war contraband by the French Government to be applied against war reparations as a result of World War I. In a series of auctions held in Paris between 1921 to 1925 a total of about $2,000,000. was realized. Today his collection would easily bring twice as much. From his holdings the famous British Guiana 1c magenta was sold to Arthur Hind for $37,500.

Arthur Hind Collection

One of the great moguls of philately was multi-millionaire textile manufacturer, Arthur Hind of Utica, N.Y. He outbid King George V of England at the Ferrary auctions for the famous British Guiana 1c magenta. His price of $37,500 made history as it was the highest ever paid for a single stamp up to that time on April 6, 1922. To-day it is estimated to be worth more than $280,000 This event which received worldwide publicity gave tremendous impetous to the savings of stamps as it stirred an enormous interest in the hobby by an aroused public. After his death in 1933, the Hind collection brought about a million dollars.

Colonel Green Collection

Colonel Edward Howland Robinson Green was the massive 290 pounds son of Hetty Green, the female wizard of Wall Street. One of his many famous purchases was the complete sheet of 24c Airmail Inverts for $20,000. After his death numerous auctions yielded an aggregate amount of over $2,850,000 for his stamps which is supposed to be the all time record for a single collection. During the height of his interest in stamps he had a full time staff employed to assist him on his philatelic work.

Maurice Burrus Collection

Maurice Burrus was formerly a resident of Lausanne, Switzerland. He was known to have had five other European residences. He will always be considered one of the all time greats among stamp collectors. Mr. Burrus was a perfectionist and no matter how rare a stamp had to be in prime condition before being accepted by him. He accumulated not one but as many superb copies of the scarcest philatelic items he could acquire. Before his death he estimated his philatelic treasures to be worth no less than $10,000,000.

Thomas K. Tapling Collection

T. K. Tapling was a wealthy British carpet manufacturer. From boyhood he was a zealous collector and student of stamps. After his death in 1891 his collection was bequeathed to the British Museum. At that time it was considered to be the largest world collection of postage stamps in existence. Mr. Tapling must be thanked for having preserved for posterity many of the rarest treasures of early issues. An estimated appraisal of $3,000,000 for this collection would not be considered too high.

Alfred Caspary Collection

Alfred H. Caspary was an important Wall Street broker and financier. As a connoisseur of philatelic classics, he specialized in rarities of only the highest quality. The result was that has collection not only surpassed any other for the number of its prize specimens but also for their high state of preservation. Since his death it has required a series of auctions to dispose of his vast collection. The total realization brought about $3,000,000.

THEODORE E. STEINWAY (PATRON OF PHILATELY)

Theodore E. Steinway (1883-1957) is not only famous for having one of the most valuable and outstanding stamp collections of his time. He is best honored for the unequalled contributions he made towards the advancement and preservation of philatelic knowledge. Although a very busy and the top executive of the world famous Steinway Piano Co. he gave generously of his time, dedication and financial support towards development of the library of the Collector's Club. Among his many and constant personal gifts were rare works on philatelic study, and research, specialized collections and literature embracing most everything connected with stamps. As a result of his achievements the library can boast of having the most complete and important storehouse of philatelic knowledge known in the world. In tribute to Mr. Steinway the Collectors Club has established in his name the Steinway Memorial Publications Fund.

Alfred Lichtenstein Collection

Was president of the Ciba Co., world famous manufacturers of dyes. He was an ardent collector as well as a perfectionist in his acquisitions. Being devoted to philately, he gave much of his time to Stamp Societies and other philatelic endeavors. He purchased the George H. Worthington collection for $500,000. His stamp collection, valued at over $3,000,000 was left to his daughter Mrs. J. D. Dale.

LOUISE BOYD DALE

Mrs. Dale was indeed a true and worthy daughter of the great philatelist, Alfred Liechtenstein from whom she inherited his love and dedication for stamps. She kept up her father's work and zeal in research and advancement of Philately. Towards that purpose she always made available her expert knowledge as well as her valuable holdings. To give an idea of the enormous worth of her stamp collection, one of the items alone fetched in auction an all time world record price of $380,000. She gave generously of her time and was very active in organization activities. Among the various philatelic societies of which she was a member are the Royal Philatelic Society, London, Roll of Distinguished Philatelists, Philatelic Foundation, Collectors Club and recipient of the Alfred F. Liechtenstein Memorial Award 1962, etc. She distinguished herself on most of these as chairman.

SOME TYCOONS OF THE STAMP TRADE

Bernard D. Harmer Henry Ellis Harris.

H. R. HARMER, INC., NEW YORK, N. Y.

Head of the New York office of this international house of distinguished stamp auctioneers is Bernard D. Harmer. He succeeded his famous father Henry R. Harmer who lived the long span of 96 years. Besides having offices in New York, the firm also has offices in London (England) and Sydney (Australia). Their clients have included Crowned Heads, Presidents, Rajahs and giants of industry. Notably among these were President Roosevelt, King George V, Arthur Hind, Maurice Burrus, Alfred F. Liechtenstein and his daughter Mrs. Louise Boyd Dale, King Farouk, Rajah of Sarawak and Alfred H. Caspary. The Harmer organization in disposing of Mrs. Dale collection, brought the world's record amount of $3,455,574 for the sale of a collection by one concern. Most of the rarest stamps have passed through their hands since they started in England in 1918. Up to now Harmer's have sold approximately $100,000,000 worth of stamps.

NOTE: During the past season H.R. Harmer, Inc. exceeded all previous records with total sales of over $6,000,000.

H.E. HARRIS & CO. BOSTON, MASS.

This large Boston stamp house has about 400 employees. Its premises occupy 77,000 square feet. It maintains a fully equipped cafeteria for its many employees. The man responsible for its great growth is Henry Ellis Harris who started the firm during his boyhood. It is claimed that the business is the largest of its kind in the world.

During 1973 the firm of H.E. Harris & Co., was taken over by the giant conglomerate General Mills for a reputed sum of $25,500,000. This reflects the big business image that philately has developed. Mr. Harris remains in a consultive capacity.

Henry Ginsberg,
present owner of Scott's

D. Hillmer acquiring Scott's 1970

Scott's

There is no name that is better known in the Stamp Fraternity than Scott's, the publisher of the so called bible of Philately—"Scott's Standard Catalog". This more than 111 year old legendary house has done business as far back as with the great grandfathers of the present generation. For that reason there cannot be avoided a measure of reverence for this firm of philatelic historical fame. Its long and active existence almost parallels the entire span of time since Philately was born.

It has changed hands seven times since it was founded by J.W. Scott in 1963. J.W. Scott sold the business to the Colman Bros. who incorporated the firm under the name of Scott Stamp and Coin Co. Ltd. In 1914 the firm was acquired by the Boston financier, Charles E. Hatfield, who turned the management over to Hugh M. Clark. In 1938, Clark assumed the full ownership. During his regime the retail division of Scott's was sold to Norman Serphos. Clark, with his wife Theresa, continued to operate the publishing part of the business which included the Catalogs, Ablums and other publications. It was he who inaugurated Scott's Monthly Journal and got out the first edition of the U.S. Specialized Catalog.

In 1946, Clark was forced to retire on account of ill health. The business was purchased by Gordon Harmer who also assumed the editorship.   He sold the business in 1960 to Esquire, Inc., but remained as editor until 1971 when he returned to his native England.

The next owner was Duane Hillmer of Graphic Publishing Co., Omaha, Nebr. who took over operations in 1970. He introduced many improvements in Scott's Publications especially in design and color. Hillmer sold Scott's to Henry Ginsberg, the international financier, who is the present owner. The persons associated with Hillmer as Jack and Bert Taub, James Hatcher, Richard Gordon and Larry Greenwald, Henry Eberle and others were kept on the staff.

SOME TYCOONS OF THE STAMP TRADE

Sam Grossman founder and president of the Grossman Stamp Co. Inc., a former President of the American Stamp Dealers' Assn. and incidentally is also author of this book.

GROSSMAN STAMP CO., IN. NEW YORK, N. Y.

The above firm may also be mentioned as one of the leading publishers and manufacturers of philatelic products. This concern was originated in 1922 by Samuel Grossman, who incidentally is the author. First operating as a part time business, the project developed over the years into an enterprise occupying the entire sixth floor of two adjoining buildings. Its sunny offices overlook Union Square which is very convenient for most all New York transit lines. The production of its world famous publications, packets and other philatelic products run into the millions.

MINKUS PUBLICATIONS, INC., NEW YORK, N. Y.

One of the leading publishers and stamp dealers in the field. The head of this enterprise is Jacques Minkus. Besides operating the Gimbel Brothers Stamp Department of New York, Mr. Minkus operates about a dozen other stamp departments throughout the leading department stores of the United States.

KURT WEISHAUPT & CO.

This firm is one of the leading importers of postage stamps. It specializes in large transactions and deals direct with some of the foreign governments. Although its operations are limited, the volume is high. Mr. Kurt Weishaupt was a former president of the American Stamp Dealers Association.

No doubt there are others who may be mentioned as important in the stamp trade as J. & H. Stolow, Fatoullah & Lazar, Inc., Harold Cohn & Co., Washington Press, Elbe File & Binder Co., Lighthouse Publications, etc. but lack of space does not permit further details.

Don Hirschhorn   J. Oliver Amos

DON HIRSCHHORN

For a success story, Don Hirschhorn cannot be overlooked. With a paltry investment of only $200.00 he started out as a peddler with his stamp merchandise stocked in the trunk of his car. His volume of business now runs into the millions. As is obvious he has built up a conglomerate comprising various important affiliations in the stamp business. Among these are Gray-Davis, Inc., Malter-Westerfield Publishing Co., Inc., Enco Nat'l Corp, H. G. Treacher & Co., Vis-A-Pak Mfg. Corp., etc. The parent company, Don Hirschhorn, Inc. was organized by him in 1952. This firm is the only publicly owned company in the stamp trade. It manufactures and distributes packets, albums, accessories, supplies, etc. to retail outlets throughout the United States. He caters to thousands of stores including the largest chains, discount houses, etc. The main quarters occupy 25,000 sq. ft. in a modern building in **OLD BETHPAGE, L.I., N.Y.** also maintains warehouses in Wisconsin and California. Hirschhorn's relations with his family of associates are close and most cordial. This applies also with other people he does business with who generally consider him of high responsibility. Don is comparatively still a young man and should still go a long way further towards becoming the top merchant in philately.

J. OLIVER AMOS (PUBLISHER)

J. Oliver Amos is the publisher of Linn's Stamp News. His cousin William T. Amos is co-publisher. Linn's Stamp News is the world's largest philatelic publication and also has the highest circulation of any periodical in Stampdom with 89,000 subscribers. Each edition has between 72 to 128 pages of tabloid size. For the aforementioned reasons it is a popular advertising medium in the stamp trade. Linn's Stamp News is a division of the Amos, Press, Inc. which was founded by Amos' grandfather in 1876. Besides "Linn's Stamp News", the Amos stable of publications includes "The Coin World" which like Linn's Stamp News is the largest weekly in its particular field.

In spite of his many interests Mr. Amos has given much dedication and time towards the advancement of Philately. An extensive traveler he champions philately at every opportunity here and abroad. He does not withhold efforts or expense to have Linn's Stamp News give the fullest coverage and services on stamps. Linn's is packed with featured articles, illustrations and contributions from the foremost columnists and authorities on stamps. Also has regular enlightening editorials of stampic interest.

Philalelic Periodical . With Raymond G. Weill and Robert A. Siegel on front cover celebrating the purchase for $34,000 by Weill of a magnificent copy of an unused copy of the 15¢ invert of the U.S. 1869 Issue.

RAYMOND H. WEILL CO.

This is a fabulous partnership made up of the brothers Raymond and Roger Weill. Their presence is usually felt whenever any of the rarest philatelic classics are put up for sale in auctions or other channels. Their colossal transactions usually make sensational world-wide headlines. With apparent disregard for costs they will in eagerness to obtain the choicest philatelic gems will generally outbid all other competitive offers. Many of their purchases have been made at record breaking prices. They operate from a moderate size store in the old French quarter of New Orleans.

Among their prize acquisitions is a U.S. 1918 block of 24c Airpost Stamps with centers inverted. For this they paid $100,000.00. On Oct. 21, 1968, the Raymond H. Weil Co., at the H.R. Harmer sale, paid a record price of $380,000.00 for a Mauritius cover with two copies of the 1947 Issue 1 penny orange with the rare Post Office Errors. This was from the collection of the late Mrs. Louise Boyd Dale. It is the highest price ever paid for a single philatelic item.

ROBERT A. SIEGEL

A dealer who during comparatively recent times has made sensational strides becoming one of the top auctioneers in stampdom is Robert A. Siegel, well known connoisseur and authority on rare and expensive U.S. stamps, etc. He occupies a suite of modern offices at 10 East 52nd St., New York. On his premises has been conducted some of the most fabulous transactions. History was made in a recent Siegel auction whereby the highest priced single stamp changed hands for the record breaking price of $280,000. In a recent single year he realized a total $4,400,000.

Although under constant business pressure he gives a liberal amount of his time to various philatelic organizations. he is a former president of the American Stamp Dealers Association. Also he is active in various welfare and charitable activities.

Linn's Weekly Stamp News

Sidney, Ohio 45365. $6.50 per year (Canada $8.50. All other coun-tires $10.50). (52 issues). Sample on request.

Mekeel's Weekly Stamp News

Box 1660, Portland, Maine 04104. $2.75 per year (Canada $3.50. Foreign $4.50) (52 issues). Sample on request.

National Stamp News

Anderson, South Carolina 29621. Published thrice a month. $5.00 per year. (Canada and foreign countries $6.00) (36 issues). Includes membership in National Philatelic Society.

Scott's Stamp Journal

604 Fifth Ave., New York, N.Y. 10020. Includes new issues and changes in catalog prices. $7.50 per year. (Canada Same) (11 issues).

Stamps Magazine

153 Waverly Place, New York, N.Y. 10014. $5.00 per year. (Canada and Latin America $6.00. Other countries $6.50) (52 issues). Sample on request.

Western Stamp Collector

P.O. Box 10, Albany, Oregon 97321. Weekly (every Saturday). $5.50 per year. (Canada same. Other countries $8.00). Sample on request.

PHILATELIC SOCIETIES AND EXHIBITS

The American Philatelic Society

Largest American Organization for Stamp collectors. Dues $10.00 annually. Includes monthly magazine, The American Philatelist. Secretary, P.O. Box 800, State College, Pa. 16801.

Society of Philatelic Americans

One of the principal philatelic organizations in the United States. Includes monthly magazine. Dues $7.00 annually. Executive Secretary Joseph M. Sousa, P.O. Box 957, Bryn Mawr, Pa. 19010.

National Philatelic Society

One of the oldest and leading philatelic societies in the United States. Dues $5.00 annually, which includes a periodical issued three times a month. Address: Secretary, P.O. Box 883, Anderson, S.C. 29621.

Collectors' Club

Has own building with largest philatelic library. Located at 22 East 35th Street, New York, N.Y. Dues $50.00 annually for resident members. $15.00 annually for non-resident members.

The Royal Philatelic Society of Canada

Annual dues are $6.00 with an additional admission for $1.00. Includes a subscription to the Canadian Philatelist—published bi-monthly. For application write to the Executive Director, Royal Philatelic Society of Canada, Box 4195, Station E, Ottawa, Canada KIS 5B2. All collectors invited.

American Topical Association

Membership 21 months $6.00. Includes magazine. Check lists available of various categories of stamps. American Topical Association, 3306 North 50th St., Milwaukee, Wis. 53216.

The American Dealers' Association, Inc.

The leading stamp dealers' organization in the United States. All members pledged to fair dealing. Secretary, 595 Madison Ave., New York, N.Y. 10022. Annual dues $75.00 for regular membership.

NEW YORK PUBLIC LIBRARY
42nd Street and Fifth Avenue, New York, N.Y.On exhibition in main lobby one of the foremost collections of United States stamps. Donated by Benjamin Kurt Miller. Consists mostly of well conditioned mint specimens with descriptions from 1845 to 1926. Open daily from 9 A.M. to 9 P.M. Saturdays from 9 A.M. to 5 P.M.

The American Philatelic Research Library
Lending library for Stamp Collectors. Membership $3.00 annually. Includes quarterly journal, "Philatelic Literature Review." Apply P.O. Box 338, State College, Pa. 16801.

National Postage Stamp Show
Sponsored by The American Stamp Dealers Association. Daniel R. Seigle, Executive Officer, 595 Madison Ave., New York, N.Y. 10022. Usually held annually in November at the Madison Square Exposition Rotunda, New York, N.Y.

United Nations Stamp Exhibit
42nd Street and East River, New York, N. Y. Covers those stamps issued by the United Nations. In basement concourse of the General Assembly Building. Free admission daily.

Smithsonian Institution's Stamp Exhibit
In Washington, D. C. Located on ground floor. Of world coverage with many rare classics. Free admission daily.

The PHILATELIC FOUNDATION
Chartered by the University of the State of New York for Philatelic study and research. Expertizing service available to all. Dues vary from $10.00. Apply to the Chairman, The Philatelic Foundation, 99 Park Ave., New York, N.Y. 10016

SMALLEST POST OFFICE IN THE WORLD
Located in a shed on the island of Gugh, population 5. Comprises only about 100 acres. It is among the Rocks in the Isles of Scully which is 30 miles off the southwestern tip of England. As a means of income it sells its local issues to summer tourists. Recently 5000 first day covers were sent out to collectors all over the world. The entire population of Gugh is made up of Dan Hick who operates the post office and four other members of his family. After use of Gugh stamps, Hick brings the covers by row boat to the nearby island of St. Agnes which has a government post office. There he uses also regular British stamps in addition to his own for the usual normal delivery.

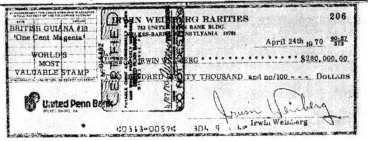

Illustrated above is the exact check for $280,000.00 which was used to pay for the British Guiana 1856 one cent magenta, the most valuable stamp in all philately.

ENJOYMENT IS THE CHIEF REWARD FOR COLLECTING STAMPS

The postage stamp collector especially of the profuse lower and medium grade stamps should not as a general rule look forward to stamps as a means of making money or as a possible fund for education or for future security. It should not be overlooked that everytime stamps are purchased the price usually includes a profit for the dealer. This is the reason why collectors are often disappointed when offering their stamps for sale to dealers. The best chance of getting back the money outlayed, or even to make some profit, would be to dispose of a stamp collection to fellow collectors who are not accustomed to buy at rock bottom trade rates. The attempt to solve this problem has been responsible for many collectors going into the stamp business.

The proper way to look upon the hobby is to consider stamps an entertainment expense just like buying tickets for the movies or a football game. This does not mean that outlays for stamps represent a complete loss or that there may not be some value or even some gain to be made. In time, when a collector emerges into advanced philately, he may then by due study of the market and careful buying, be more capable of making his purchases much more sound from an investment point of view.

Stamps As An Investment

Just as in most other commodities the values of stamps are based upon the law of supply and demand. It is not to be denied that opportunity, chance and luck have something to do with making money in stamps. However, there are certain elementary principles that anybody looking to make profits in stamps should be aware of. First nobody should rush in and buy blindly anything that comes their way. Any intelligent individual should know that if too many of any stamp are printed or if too many people grab up a certain issue, the chances for profit within a reasonable time are poor. Also, one should not be too easily swayed towards heavy buying during a wave of popularity of a certain issue. Too often, stamps popular today are forgotten tomorrow. You cannot go to the post office and buy up a lot of commemoratives or other stamps and expect to make a quick profit. It must be realized that there are thousands of other people with the same idea. Yes, there have been big profits and fortunes made in stamps but many were made under favorable conditions when perhaps issues were more limited, money scarcer or the public not so alerted as it is today to such possibilities.

RAREST STAMP SOLD FOR $280,000

History was made on March 24, 1970 at a sale of the Robert A. Siegel Auction Galleries. Due to the large attendance estimated at 700, it was necessary to use the Grand Ballroom of the Waldorf Astoria Hotel. The most famous and rarest gem of Philately was sold for $280,000 which is a record breaking price for a single stamp. This is undoubtedly the most expensive piece of paper of its kind in the world. It only took about 2 minutes for the auctioneer Andrew Levitt to conclude the sale. Together with the spectators there was an army of newsmen and cameramen made up from the Press and Television. Mr. Weinberg the successful bidder represented a syndicate of investors. The sum of $280,000. is indeed a great leap in price for this rarity which previously sold in 1940 for $45,000.

BRITISH GUIANA PAIR SOLD FOR $180,000

Ths rare pair of 1951 British Guiana circular "COTTON REELS" on envelope was sold at Robson Lowe sale in London on March 26, 1970 for £75,000. or equivalent to $180,000.

War Started By A Stamp Issue

In 1900 the Dominican Republic issued a set of stamps showing its boundary extending into the territory of its neighbor, Haïti. This started intermittent border conflicts between the two republics until 1938 when the dispute was finally settled. It is estimated that over 15,000 were slain because of this controversy.

Stamps Were Responsible for the Panama Canal Location

Before the Panama route was selected for a proposed canal to join the Atlantic and Pacific Oceans there was a faction in Washington favoring the route through Nicaragua. However an advocate of Panama distributed among the senators a Nicaraguan 1902 stamp showing that country's volcano of Mt. Momotombo and brought out that this volcano was in constant eruption and therefore a menace to the proposed waterway. This settled the issue in favor of Panama.

Tin Can Mail

This was mail sealed in a five-gallon can and thrown overboard. It was thereupon picked up by canoe or a swimmer and brought to its destination, the island of Niuafoo of the Tonga group. The mails to the steamer was by same means. This practice was discontinued due to casualties suffered by swimmers in the shark-infested waters.

Centenario de Santo Antonio
MCXCV ✱ MDCCCXCV

O lingua benedicta, quae Do-
minum semper benedixisti et
alios benedicere docuisti: nunc
perspicue cernitur quanti meriti
fueris apud Deum.

S. Boaventura.

Twenty-four cent invert   Prayer stamp (the front)   Prayer stamp (the back)

UNITED STATES 24c INVERTED AIRMAIL STAMP
$24.00 INVESTMENT NOW WORTH $4700,000

A wide-awake observer by the name of William T. Robey was at a post office window and noticed the buyer in front of him turn back to the clerk a sheet of 100 twenty-four cent airmail stamps because they were by error printed with the airplane upside down. How his heart must have throbbed when he saw within his grasp a golden opportunity to reap a fortune. He thereupon prevailed upon the uninformed clerk to let him have the sheet, which was to make philatelic history. Mr. robey disposed of this to Mr. Eugene Klein, a Philadelphia stamp dealer, who in turn sold the sheet to the late Colonel E. Green for $20,000. The colonel just kept some of the blocks he was interested in and let the single copies of the inverts go for $250 each. By 1956 the value of each stamp had risen from $250 to $47,000. On this basis the value of the original sheet has shot shot up to $4,700,000.

Prayer Stamps

Refers to 1895 Issue of Portugal, commemorating the seventh centenary of the birth of St. Anthony of Padua. All these stamps have a prayer in Latin printed on the back.

Schumann error

Schumann Reissue

Error of the Wronq Music

On July 20, 1956, the East German Government issued a set of two different stamps in honor of the composer, Robert Schumann (1810-1856). Soon thereafter it was discovered that the notes of music printed on the stamps as part of the design were by Franz Schubert, the Austrian composer, rather than by Schumann. This aroused world-wide laughter as well as consternation in the department of culture of the Government. The stamps were immediately recalled and replaced with new stamps with the right music notes.

A great and unique rarity. Block of Four 24c United States 1918 Airpost stamps with the airplane centers inverted. (upside down) Previously acquired for $100,000 by Weill Bros. of New Orleans. Since then the purchase of just a single stamp of this invert was sold for $47,000. Therefore the block should be worth now over $200,000.

FABULOUS U. S. CLASSICS
PAN AMERICAN 1901 Issue with inverted centers

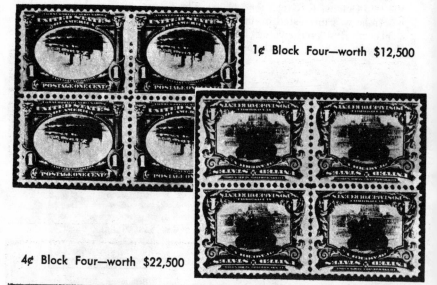

1¢ Block Four—worth $12,500

4¢ Block Four—worth $22,500

2¢ PAN AMERICAN INVERT

The rarest invert of the series.

Single copy—Worth $12,000
Block four—Worth $50,000

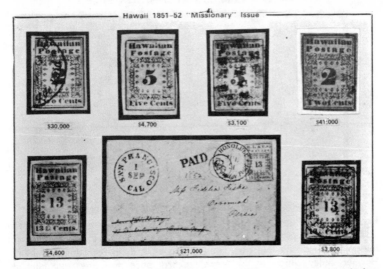

$30,000 $4,700 $3,100 $41,000

$4,600 $21,000 $3,800

Prices realized in an auction of Hawaiian Missionary stamps including the record breaking price of $41,000 for a superb copy of the very rare 2¢ blue. Courtesy of the H. R. Harmer Organization

BROUGHT $26,000 IN AUCTION

An extremely rare and unique strip of five 4¢ brown coils. With Schermack private perforations. Purchased by Weill.

1893 Columbus unused 4¢ Plate Number strip of four. Imprint on bottom. With rare error in color. (deep blue) Sold for $12,500.

CONSIDERED THE WORLD'S GREATEST PHILATELIC GEM.
BRINGS $380,000 AT AUCTION SALE

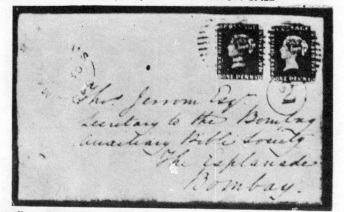

Unusually excellent Mauritius cover with two superlative copies of the 1847 Issue, 1¢ penny orange with the rare POST OFFICE ERRORS. From the collection of the late Mrs. Louise Boyd Dale. Sold for $380,000 at H. R. Harmer Sale, which is the world record price for any philatelic item. Formerly purchased for $250.00

STAMP INSURANCE

All risk insurance for the protection of stamp collections is available to members of the American Philatelic Society. Detailed information about individual policies at special rates. Apply to Executive Secretary, American Philatelic Society, P. O. Box 300, State College, Pa. 16801.

DR. WLADISLAW KOLAKOWSKI   H.R. Harmer (see page 126)

A contributing as well as an ardent Philatelist. He reflects in person and charm his aristocratic background. Descended from the Polish nobility. His family had close ties with past Polish rulers including the heroic John Sobieski (John III). Recipient of many high honors, citations and degrees of international scope. Distinguished in the fields of sciences and humanities. Ambassador extraordinary and plenipotenciary of the O.S.J.H. Knights of Malta. In charge of the Polish Philatelic Agency in the U.S.A.

Franklin D. Roosevelt   Irwin Weinberg

Franklin D. Roosevelt Collection

As president of the United States he was responsible for more inspiration and encouragment in the collecting of postage stamps than any other individual. He was a devoted collector and always claimed that stamps gave him the much needed relaxation that was required in his many trying daily duties. Auctions brought about $250,000 for his stamps but many of the items brought more than their actual worth for sentimental and prestige worth. President Roosevelt is claimed to have entirely designed some of the United States stamps. One of these is the 1933 Admiral Byrd Antarctic Expedition 3c stamp.

IRWIN WEINBERG

A new contender has emerged in the scramble for the choicest treasures of Stampdom. Hail Irwin Weinberg who victoriously outbid the strongest competitors to corner the rarest jewel in Philately. He paid the all time top price of $280,000 for a single stamp. This was for the rare 1856 British Guiana 1¢ magenta at the Robert A. Siegel Auction Galleries on March 24, 1970. At the same sale he also acquired at a new record price of $34,000 the 24¢ U.S. bicolored invert. Another notable acquisition was the 30¢ U.S. 1869 issue with flags inverted. He expects these values to double in 10 years.

Mr. Weinberg represents a group of business men who are interested in converting their money into sound investments as a protection against inflation. Mr. Weinberg is owner of the Miner Stamp Co. of Wilkes Barre, Pa. He is also connected with Irwin Weinberg Rarities of the same town with classic stamps as their specialty.

JOHN J. BRITT

John J. Britt, internationally known philatelist has a long and distinguished stamp career that represents an endless chronicle of outstanding achievements with every conceivable award and honor that Philately can bestow. He is endowed with a dynamic drive from which Philately has been one of the chief beneficiaries. When this is harnessed to any philatelic undertaking there, is bound to be plenty of action. Among the important organizations which he has served as President, are the Collectors Club of N. Y., Aero Philatelists and The Association for Stamp Exhibitions. He has been closely associated with such giants of Philately as Alfred F. Lichtenstein, Theodore E. Steinway, Clarence W. Brazer and Gen. C. W. Wickersham.

Due to his high reputation as an authority on stamps in general as well as being an eloquent speaker, he is much sought after to act as Chairman, Master of Ceremonies, as well as a judge at philatelic exhibitions. He also willingly gives his time to public welfare projects and fund raising campaigns at which he is most effective.

Besides his philatelic interests he is Chief Supervisor for the New York State Board of Law Examiners. Philately however is his first love. However it is his inclination to have the thrills and blessings of stamp collecting shared with others. In that direction, he has with other highly spirited philatelists founded the 'School of Philately' in Hollywood, Florida.

In addition to his many affiliations, he is a Fellow of the Royal Philatelic Society, London, England. On June 1, 1974 a trust named the John J. Britt Philatelic Foundation for the donor was created for the furtherance of philatelic knowledge and to promote and encourage the collecting of stamps among the public. Also to provide incentives and awards at local and national philatelic exhibitions. The stamp fraternity certainly owes Mr. Britt a great debt of gratitude for his consistent and unselfish efforts in behalf of and the spreading of our hobby. There are few devotees in Stampdom that could match his zeal and affection for Stamps. This is besides frequently putting his hands in his pocket to help the cause.

Hollywood (Florida) School of Philately. Front row officers (l-r): William Hogeland, George Blizil, John Britt, Kenneth Luxenberg, John Rider. (photo by David E. Glenn, No. Miami)

THE SCHOOL OF PHILATELY

This is a non-profit affiliate of the Hollywood Stamp Club, Hollywood, Fla. Member Murray Kramer is credited with the idea. It was put into reality by a highly spirited group of executives including John J. Britt, Board Chairman, George A. Blizil, Samuel Stewart, Wm. H. Hogeland, J. Leonard Diamond, Kenneth Luxenberg, M.D., Col. John F. Rider. It is voluntarily financed through contributions from a group of trustees. There are no tuition fees. Each student receives free everything necessary to collect stamps, including albums, stamps, manuals, reference material, accessories, essential supplies and even refreshments. It is with much pride to this publisher that the school has adopted as a textbook our "Stamp Collectors Handbook". There has also been organized by the school a junior stamp club for Negro youngsters. It is believed to be the first such group in the nation.

Sessions take place weekly at the Hollywood Recreation Center, 2030 Polk St., Hollywood, Fla. Efforts to increase the attendance is made through door prizes and other inducements. All this is also free. Prominent Philatelists and authorities volunteer to give instructions at no charge and at their own expense. In addition to the fundamentals of stamp collecting, lessons are also given on the proper use of Philatelic Utensils, Handling, Removing Stamps, What to Collect, Postal History, selection and care of Albums including lettering, etc. At the last count there were 116 students registered for the 20 week course, 48 were women. Upon the completion of the course a student is awarded at graduation ceremonies a gold seal certificate.

In honor to the school the Mayor of Hollywood, Maynard Abrams, by proclamation declared "A Week of Philately." The local newspapers and radio station here also gave good publicity and support to the school.

143

GEORGE SILBERBERG

Here is an individual who has dedicated his entire life and efforts to the alleviation of the unfortunates. In doing this he uses stamps as one of his principal mediums of dispensing widespread joy and happiness among the countless recipients of his generosity.

He heads a group called Philatelic Hobbies for the Wounded and Hobbies for all Ages. He is also an honored member and First Vice President of the Grand Street Boys Ass'n. Through the facilities of these and other organizations with whom he is widely associated he stretches out a helping hand to the Crippled, the Aged, Wounded War Veterans, Penal Institutions, Salvation Army, Police Athletic Club and other Youth Groups, Recreation Centers, etc.

From his large warehouse and distribution center known as Hobby-craft Headquarters at 2122 Wallace Avenue, Bronx, N. Y. 10462 he distributes Stamps, Hobbycraft Items as well as other goods as Clothing, Shoes, Toys, Books and numerous other useful items. This may be done right at our doorstep or as far out as the remote Pitcairn Is.

His venture was inspired from a hospital bed. Through an accident both his legs were crushed and he faced a dark future as a helpless invalid. He swore that if he recovered he would spend the rest of his life helping the needy. His recovery was complete and his grateful spirit has served mankind ever since.

To give an idea of the magnitude and benevolence of his crusade there has been since 1952 more than 575,000 cartons of material distributed by him through more than 3700 institutions. To date $26,000,000 of new merchandise has been distributed. The value is only based on 25% of the true worth. Besides over 175 awards and citations have been made by Government and private organizations attesting to Silverberg's admirable endeavors for mankind. Everything is done on a voluntary basis including donations and the personnel handling the operations. Contributions are always welcome of Stamps, Albums, Accumulations, etc. Phone TA 9-4847. (Area Code 212)

SUPPLEMENTARY PHILATELIC TERMS

Refer to INDEX for possible further information on subjects that follow. Also refer to INDEX for other subjects not included below.

ADHESIVE

The term adhesive distinguishes stamps intended for attachment by gummed back or outside means from those printed or embossed directly on envelope, wrapper, letter sheet, postal card or other form of postal stationery.

ADVERTISEMENTS (TABS)

Used by governments for propaganda and communal purposes. Also by private interests with the sanction of the government. These may be either on the backs of the stamps or on the side.

ALBINO

A colorless impression of an entire stamp. This being done in the process of embossing but accidentally without ink. Occurs mostly with envelope stamps.

ALLIED MILITARY GOVERNMENT ISSUES (A.M.G.)

Usually referred to as A.M.G. Issues. These are stamps issued jointly by U.S. and Great Britain during and after World War II in occupation areas under their control, as in Austria, France, Germany and Italy.

AMERICAN BANK NOTE COMPANY

A private firm which under contract with the U.S. Post Office printed the 1879-94 Issues. Also printed stamps for Canada and other foreign countries. Amalgamated in 1879 with the National Bank Note Co. and the Continental Bank Note Co.

APPROVAL CARDS

These are usually 3 x 5½ inch stiff Manila cards with three pockets to each running across. Into these pockets stamps can be inserted or withdrawn with ease. Pockets may be or not be transparent. Very convenient for stockkeeping, trade, duplicates, etc.

APPROVAL SELECTIONS

A convenient method by which a dealer sends selections of stamps to prospective purchasers. This may be either on sheets, in booklets, envelopes, etc. Under each stamp or set is marked the price which may be either net or subject to a flat discount. From these sendings the collector selects what he wants and with his remittance he returns the balance of the stamps. Sometimes a dealer will make a special price if the entire selection is taken.

AUCTIONS

An important practice in disposing of stamps. Descriptions of the lots and catalog value are usually furnished to prospects. Bids are received through mail or at session of auctioneers sale, or by both methods.

B.M.A.

Overprinted on British Colonial stamps. Abbreviated for British Military Administration.

BALLOON POSTS

These were among the earliest attempts to send mail by air. The most famous achievement in this direction was the balloon posts resorted to by besieged Paris in 1870. This was the only means to send messages to the outside world.

BATTLESHIPS

Relating to the United States 1898 Documentary and Proprietary Revenue Issues with illustration of the battleship Maine.

BICENTENNIAL ISSUES

Such described issues refer to the 200th anniversary. An excellent example of these are the U.S. 1932 Washington Bicentennial Commemoratives.

BI-LINGUAL STAMPS

Where two or more languages are used for descriptions on stamps. Typical examples will be found among stamps of Union of South Africa, South-West Africa, Belgium, New Hebrides and Palestine.

BISECT

A stamp that has been cut in half with each half used as a separate stamp at one half the value of the original unseparated copy. This is brought about when there is a shortage of stamps. Such specimens are recognized as authentic by some philatelists only if on the actual cover with the postmark over both the shortened stamp and adjacent space. Bisects may be diagonal half, horizontal half or vertical half.

BLACK JACKS

Pet name for the United States 2 cent black Jackson stamps, 1863-75 Issues.

BOURSE

A gathering of collectors and stamp dealers for the purpose of buying, selling and the exchanging of stamps.

Broken hat

BROKEN HAT

Refers to certain of the United States 1893 2-cent Columbus stamps in which the hat of the discoverer has a visible gash due to a defect in the plate.

BULL'S EYE

Refers to the first issue of Brazil 1843. So called due to the eyeshaped design of the stamps.

BUNDLE WARE

This is the technical term for describing stamps which have been washed free from paper, assorted and put up in bundles of 100. Such units may also be held together by bands, threads, envelopes. etc. This is a common term in the trade with dealers handling cheap wholesale material in large quantity especially for packets, mixtures and approvals.

BUREAU ISSUES

United States stamps issued by the Bureau of Engraving and Printing in Washington, D.C. May also be applicable to precancels which have been overprinted by the Bureau.

CANTONALS
Nickname for stamps issued by the Cantonal Administration of Switzerland between 1843-50. These were succeeded by those of the federal government.

CARLIST
Refers to the 1873-5 issue of Spain which was printed by Don Carlos, the self-appointed king. The issues however were only in partial use in Spain.

CARRIERS' STAMPS
Used during the early period when the ordinary postage fee provided for delivery of mail only from post office to post office. By use of a carrier's stamp, the delivery of the mail was extended from post office to addressee.

CASE HARDENING
A means of coating printing plates with chrome or nickel. Will enable them to stand heavy use. Plates may be re-coated as necessary and thereby be used indefinitely.

CATAPULT MAIL
In early stages of aviation, this was a ship-to-shore service by airplane, expediting the delivery of mail. With the improvement of Trans-Atlantic airmail, this service was no longer necessary.

CENSORED MAIL
Resorted to during peace or war as a means of defense against espionage and to safeguard vital information. After examination, a special censor-marked seal or mending paper was used to close the envelope.

CENTENARY
Such described issues refer to the hundredth anniversary.

CIGARETTE TUBE REVENUE STAMPS (U. S.)
Used for collection of taxes on the commodity as specified. These will be found listed in Scott's United States Specialized Catalog.

CIVIL WAR REVENUES (UNITED STATES)
Applies to United States Revenue Stamps, 1862-71 Issues. These were utilized to help defray expenses of the Civil War.

CLEANED PLATE

After constant use, a plate may become clogged with ink and thereby reduce the sharpness in printing. After such a plate undergoes a thorough cleaning the impressions from the cleaned plate should show a distinct difference than heretofore.

COLONIALS (or COLONIES)

This term is usually combined with the name of the mother country as British Colonies, French Colonies, etc. Philatelically this may include the issues of countries which formerly were colonies but have since become sovereign states with independent issues.

CLASSICS

Refers particularly to 19th Century Stamps which due to background, rarity, excellence of design or popularity have earned outstanding respect from philatelists. Among the aristocrats are British Guiana 1856 1 cent magenta, the Mauritius errors, Hawaiian Missionaries, United States 1847 5 cent brown and 10 black, Great Britain 1p black, Cape of Good Hope triangles, etc. Also a good percentage of the scarcer 19th Century United States stamps can qualify for this category.

COMMEMORATIVES

These are special issues for the express purpose of honoring a certain person, event, anniversary or group. These are usually issued only for a limited time. They are not intended to supplant regular issues but are sold concurrently with them.

CONDOMINIUM

A territory controlled or administered by two countries. New Hebrides is a typical example.

CONFEDERATE STATES, PROVISIONAL ISSUES

Stamps and envelopes issued by the postmasters of various Southern towns from the discontinuance of Federal issues after the secession up to the time of the first Confederate issue. Further use of Provisionals were made where supply of government stamps was exhausted.

CONSULAR SERVICE STAMPS

In referring to United States Revenue Stamps, it signifies a charge by a consulate abroad for a service rendered. Listed in Scott's United States Specialized Catalog.

CONTINENTAL BANK NOTE COMPANY

This firm printed under government contract the United States 1873 Issue. Its predecessor, the National Bank Note Co., made some slight variations on the printing dies before turning them over to the new printing firm. This brought about the famous Secret Marks.

COMPARATIVE DETAILS: Inside the ball to left of the numeral one, there has been added a small curved line.

CORONATIONS

Applies to the British Empire. This denotes a series of issues used throughout the British Empire in 1937 in honor of the ascendancy to the throne of George VI and also for that of Queen Elizabeth II in 1953.

CONVENTION STATES (of INDIA)

States of India which used the regular stamps of British India surcharged with their respective names. These were valid for postage throughout all of India. Among those under this status were Chamba, Gwalior, Faridkot, Jhind, Nabha and Patiala.

CORDIALS AND WINE STAMPS (U.S.)

Used to facilitate the collection of taxes on the aforementioned liquors. Listed in Scott's United States Specialized Catalog.

CORNER LETTERS

Small letters in the corner of the early issues of Great Britain which were not only a safeguard against theft and forgery but were also a check on distribution.

COVERS

These are divided into various categories. First, they must all be complete entires and bear proof of having served postal duty. Those with old emissions on cover, especially 19th Century U. S. stamps, are usually more valuable with the stamps than with the stamps off. Hence it is always advisable not to remove stamps from envelopes without first ascertaining the values. Also see Postal Stationery, First Day Covers, First Flight Covers, Patriotic Covers, Valentine Covers, etc.

CRACKED PLATE

Refers to stamps showing signs that the plate utilized for printing was cracked. These are usually in the form of irregular lines running under the strain in various directions. Considered a flaw.

Cracked plate.

CURRENT STAMPS

Stamps are considered current if in present use.

DEATH MASK STAMPS

These refer to the first five values of the 1904 set of Serbia which have the dual profiles of Karegeorge (Serbian patriot) and King Peter I. By turning these stamps upside down there will be revealed between the profiles a deathmask which is claimed to be from the head of the previously murdered King Alexander. This is considered purely accidental.

DEFINITIVE ISSUE

The regular series of stamps in general use over a period as distinguished from those of only temporary, provisional or commemorative use.

DEMONETIZED STAMPS

When unused stamps are no longer acceptable for use on mail, they are termed demonetized.

Ordinary: one amount.   With Surtax. 25c + 10c.

DENOMINATION

The amount of the face value appearing on a stamp. On ordinary stamps this is indicated by one amount. However on such stamps as semi-postal issues there may be a surtax in addition to the regular postage, so there will be **two** denominations. The total of the two is the cost or face value of the stamp.

DEPARTMENTS (OFFICIALS)

The name usually given to United States 1873-79 Official Issues when the various branches or departments of the government had their own separate stamps. Those included the Departments of Agriculture, Executive, Interior, Justice, Navy, Post Office, State, Treasury and War.

DOCUMENTARY REVENUE STAMPS (U. S.)

To raise revenue on documents, deeds, contracts and miscellaneous other business instruments. On Civil War Documentary 1862-71 issues the stamps had inscribed the specific document or article for which it was intended.

DOUBLE IMPRESSION

Refers to an accidental second impression in printing being made by mistake over the first impression. Caused by a sheet of stamps going through the press twice. This is an error in printing and not a defect in the plate.

DOUBLE STRIKE

Applies to electrotypes or sterotypes whereby part or all of the design is impressed twice. This is caused by a shift during the implanting of the die upon the mould from which the plate is made.

DUPLICATES

The excess number of an identical stamp.

DUTY PLATE (See HEAD PLATE)

EMISSION

Another word for a stamp or issue.

ENCASED POSTAGE STAMPS

Stamps enclosed in a container substituted for currency. Used during times of coin shortage as in Civil War days.

ETCH

To engrave by biting out with acid a design previously drawn with an etching needle. By this process the area forming the design in the plate during manufacture is not affected, but the other parts are eaten away. The latter areas appear blank on the printed impression.

EXPERTIZE

To submit a stamp to an authority qualified to examine and pass judgment on that particular kind of an item.

Although stamps in the above individual groups are similar there are visible (or face) diferences.

FACE DIFFERENT

Refers to total count in an assortment of all different stamps restricted to only those of visible major varieties and excluding varieties representing minor differences such as watermarks, perforations and any other unnoticeable variations.

Normal face value ½c.   Changed by surcharge to ¼a

FACE VALUE

The value of a stamp as indicated by the denomination thereon or as changed by surcharge. If there is a surtax for charity, etc., that also is included as part of the face value. In foreign stamps the value is determined by its worth in U. S. funds according to exchange rates.

FAMOUS AMERICANS

Refers to the United States 1940 issue comprising a series of seven different sets of five varieties each. Total 35 different stamps. These sets respectively honor American authors, poets, educators, scientists, composers, artists and inventors.

FARLEY ISSUES

A special printing in 1935 for the public of certain United States commemoratives. This was in order to satisfy protests of collectors who had protested the action of the postmaster general, James A. Farley in first issuing only a limited number of these imperforates to a favored few. See also Special Printing.

FISCALS

These especially pertain to stamps which are alike or resemble postal issues but are identified as revenue (or fiscal) stamps through their cancellations such as penmarks, numerals, violet oblongish (elliptical) circles, etc. Scott's limits the listings of fiscal issues to just those of the United States. The foreign revenues are generally excluded by postage stamp collectors. See also Postal Fiscals.

FLAGS

Among United States issues this refers to the 1943-4 issue whereby in which thirteen different stamps were issued with the flags of overrun countries.

FLAT PLATE PRINTING

Applies to stamps printed from presses having flat plates as distinguished from cylinder plates used on rotary presses.

FRAME

The outer portion of a stamp within which is the central design, portrait or other subject.

UNITED STATES
GOVERNMENT PRINTING OFFICE
DIVISION OF PUBLIC DOCUMENTS
WASHINGTON 25, D. C.
———
OFFICIAL BUSINESS

PENALTY FOR PRIVATE USE TO AVOID
PAYMENT OF POSTAGE, $300
(GPO)

FRANKS (FREE)

The privilege of sending mail free. This right is usually indicated on the envelope through form of printed permission, official signature, label, etc. Largely utilized by government departments, congressmen, senators, the military service, etc.

FUGITIVE INKS

Inks which dissolve when moistened in water or other fluids.

FUTURE DELIVERY (U. S.)

Applies to United States revenue stamps. Used for collection of taxes on sale or agreement for sale at any exchange or other trade board for future delivery.

FUTURE

DELIVERY

GENERAL COLLECTOR

One who collects stamps of all countries.

GENERAL ISSUES.

Also known as the regular and ordinary issues. These are stamps issued for all mail purposes as distinguished from those used specifically for only airpost, parcel post, officials, special delivery or any other of the special postal services.

GOVERNMENT-IN-EXILE ISSUES

Refers to those issues of governments which because of invasion or defeat, have been forced to vacate their native country and set themselves up in an allied or neutral country. Examples of such issues were Netherlands 1944-5 and Norway 1943-5. The latter issues during the war were mostly aboard ships and after liberation continued as general issues. There have been other so called government-in-exile issues such as anti-Nazi, anti-Communist and Revolutionary. Some of these have been and are still very controversial over status and recognition. It may take years before a standard catalog may recognize such an issue by insertion or even remove an issue after insertion.

GRAVER (or BURIN)

The engraver's cutting instrument. Has sharp steel blade with wooden handle.

GUIDE LINES

These are horizontal or vertical lines (colored) on the sheets to aid in proper perforation of the stamps and the separation of the sheet into panes.

GUIDE DOTS

Placed on the plate before it is engraved. The express purpose is to guide transfers of the design to the new plate into the correct positions. After these guide dots have served their purpose they are usually removed but if overlooked they may show in the printing.

HABILITADO

Spanish word. Indicates that a discontinued issue has been made valid again for postage.

HAND-STAMPED ISSUES

Among the earlier issues a number of stamps were impressed on the envelopes direct from a die attached to a handle, in the same manner as a rubber stamp. This distinguishes such issues from those printed by machinery. Surcharges have been likewise applied.

Head (or Key) Plate   Duty Plate

HEAD (or KEY) PLATE

Of the two plates used in bi-colored printing, as in the case of key types of British Colonies and Portuguese Colonial stamps, this is the plate that has the portrait. This usually includes as well the inscribed frame and general design used through the entire series.

The other plate used in bi-colored printing of key type issues is known as the duty plate. It usually bears the name of the country, denomination, etc.

HUNTING PERMIT STAMPS

Applies to United States Revenue Stamps. Issued for limited period to licensed hunters. The revenue received is utilized for the protection nad conservation of wild birds and game.

INFLATION STAMPS OR ISSUES

These are stamps issued during the collapse of a country's currency. The best known example of these are the German 1921-3 Inflation Issues, when the denominations soared to as high as 50 billion marks. Among other countries which had inflation issues are Austria, Hungary, Poland, Romania, Russia, various Russian states, Greece, China, etc.

IMPRINTS

This usually refers to the name of the printer often found on the margin of a sheet of stamps or underneath stamps.

INSCRIPTION

The wordings including title and other text on a stamp.

INTERLEAVING

A transparent sheet, usually glassine, which is inserted between leaves. Acts as a protective covering over the stamps. Usually can be purchased in standard sizes and attached to posts of binders like album sheets.

INTERNATIONAL REPLY COUPONS

Coupons issued by the authority of the Universal Postal Union for use by its affiliated countries. This is to provide return postage for a correspondent in a foreign country. In addition to language of issuing country, it has instructions printed on reverse side in various other languages.

JUBILEE STAMPS

Indicates a specific anniversary or celebration.

KANSAS - NEBRASKA OVERPRINTS

Because of numerous thefts from post offices in the states of Kansas and Nebraska, stocks of stamps in these two states were overprinted respectively with "Kans" and "Nebr." Stamps so overprinted were not acceptable in any other states which made it difficult for the disposel of the stolen stamps.

LETTER SHEET

May refer to the early folded letter with or without stamps or to recent types with stamps especially for airpost use.

LOCALS

Private or official posts operable only within a town, muncipality, district or otherwise restricted area. Such stamps are not valid for postage outside of the confines of the locality. Some local issues have been counterfeited or reprinted to abuse and therefore caution should be exercised in acquiring original specimens.

MAJOR VARIETIES

Variations of importance in the features or designs of stamps including denominations, color, inscriptions.

MANDATE ISSUES

Stamps issued for a country or territory held in mandate as a result of a war, or in trust awaiting peace treaty for disposition. Examples are Tanganyika and Togo.

MATCH AND MEDICINE STAMPS (U. S.)

Of Private Proprietary Issues. Issued in 19th Century with government sanction as revenue stamps for collection of taxes on patented medicine, matches, perfumery and other products. The stamps were affixed on boxes, bottles, containers, etc.

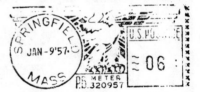

METERED MAIL

This is a machine which under government permit makes printed impressions of prepaid postage. These are deducted by meter against money advanced to the post office for postage. The design of the impression is known as an indicia or meter mark. Other advantages of this machine are that it seals as well as franks mail matter, is a protection against theft and expediates delivery as no time is spent in canceling stamps. Also permits use of advertising matter or slogans with the printed meter impressions.

MINOR ISSUES

Refers mostly to stamp issues of specialized and limited services. Consequently they are usually less profuse in number as well as in popularity. For these reasons albums, catalogs, etc., intended for ordinary collectors may omit minor issues such as registration stamps, acknowledgment of receipt stamps, newspaper stamps, late fee stamps, etc.

Stamps printed on backs. Valid either as postage or currency.

MONEY STAMPS

Emissions as for instance Russia 1915-7 card stamps which were valid both for postage and small currency. France between 1914 to 1918 also utilized stamps as currency; likewise Rhodesia in times of emergency. Also see Encased Stamps.

MOURNING STAMPS

Stamps issued out of respect or in memory of deceased individuals of importance such as leaders of state, etc. It is typical of these emissions to have the edges in black. Common examples are Jugoslavia 1934 King Alexander mourning stamps, Germany 1934 Hindenberg mourning stamps, etc. Personages of great international repute like Franklin D. Roosevelt have been honored by mourning stamps from a multitude of foreign countries.

MINOR VARIETIES

These represent slight variations in the basic features of stamps. In this category may be variations in perforations, watermarks, secret marks, colors, shades and tints, paper, re-engraved lines and other generally unnoticeable face differences. This can be stretched without limit depending upon what lengths advanced collectors and specialists will go to in philatelic research.

NATIVE STATES OF INDIA

These states which have had or still retain the right to issue their own distinct stamps for use within their borders with only the exception of Cochin and Travencore which have a mutual postal agreement.

NATIONAL BANK NOTE CO., (U. S.)

Printed under government contract the United States 1870-1 Issues. (See also Continental Bank Note Co.)

NEW ISSUES

Stamps recently issued. Price lists of such issued by stamp dealers generally cover stamps issued during the past six months.

NEW ISSUE SERVICE

A special arrangement maintained by some stamp dealers whereby subscribers to this service are supplied with future new issues according to preferences, quantity, limitations on face values and other specifications, per contract.

NEWSPAPER AND PERIODICAL STAMPS (U. S.)

Issued between 1865-99. These stamps have been discontinued in the United States since then. Used as prepayment of postage on bulk shipments. The stamps were attached to mailing receipts, cancelled and retained by the post office.

OFFICES ABROAD (POST OFFICES ABROAD)

These are post offices which are or have been maintained by various countries in consulates abroad. Such stamps are usually the regular types of their respective countries but are overprinted with the name of the post office town. Another country like France had a distinct standard key type stamp which applied to all such offices. Aside from the different names of the various offices, the design of the stamp was the same throughout.

ON COVER

Indicates that the stamp is still attached to the envelope as received through the mail.

ORDINARY MAIL STAMPS

The regular mail stamps for general all purpose use.

O.H.M.S.

Abbreviation for On His (or Her) Majesty's Service. Frequently used on British Colonial official stamps.

OBSOLETE STAMPS

Stamps so described indicate that they are no longer for sale at the post office. However in the event that these stamps are no longer acceptable for use even as postage they are therefore considered as demonetized.

PACKETS

Represents a quantity of stamps put up in an individual envelope. The latter may be plain, have a window, be illustrated, and have its contents described. The term packet implies that all stamps therein are different which may technically include minor variations such as watermarks, shades, perforations, printing processes, etc. However, where it is indicated that the contents are all face different it is understood that the contents are made up of only major or visibly different stamps.

PEACE ISSUES (BRITISH EMPIRE)

A series of issues issued throughout the British Empire in celebration of the restoration of peace after close of World War II.

PENNY BLACK

Pet name for the first adhesive postage stamp. This is the one penny black portrait of Queen Victoria issued by Great Britain in 1840.

PERFORATED (INITIALED) STAMPS

Also known as punctured stamps. These have initials perforated into body of stamp. This is to trace as well as avoid thefts.

PERMITS (U. S. POST OFFICE)

This covers metered mail, precancels, bulk mail, paid postage and other classifications of mail matter for which a special permit must be obtained from the post office. Also applies to some foreign countries.

PHILATELY

Philately is a Greek word derived from philos (fond of) and ateles (free of tax, prepaid). The name was first coined by the French collector, Herpin. The more modern version would be, the collecting, study and advancement of postage stamps and other stamped matter of related nature.

PHILATELIST

The more serious type of collector and student of postage stamps.

PHILATELIC AGENCY

A service established by the United States Government to make available to stamp collector at face value any issue it may have in stock. To the purchase price must be added postage and insurance. For complete list write to the Philatelic Agency, Post Office Dept., Washington, D.C. The Philatelic Agency maintains another office at the New York General Post Office, 33rd St. and 8th Ave., New York, N. Y.

PIGEON POSTS

This method by far pre-dates our present systems. The ancients including the Greeks and Romans utilized pigeon posts. In more recent times Pigeon Posts have been used and still occasionally used during siege, in inaccessable territory, in isolated Arctic outposts, in times of emergency and as regular posts.

PILLARS

The printing matter in the margins between panes, etc. of a sheet to prevent the blank parts from being used for counterfeiting.

PICTORIAL

A stamp so described should bear as its chief design a subject of scenic, structural or other illustrative matter which can be construed as picturesque. This should preclude such stamps that have for their principal design, numerals, individual portraits, ordinary symbols like eagles, coats of arms etc.

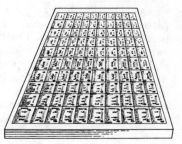

PLATE (GENERAL)

In modern printing refers to a flat or cylinder metal sheet from which stamps are printed. Former printing processes also utilized wood and stone as printing plates (or blocks).

PLATE NUMBER

The number usually seen on the margin of a sheet or pane of stamps. The purpose is for identification of the plate.

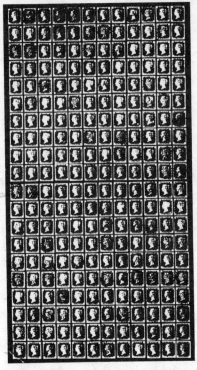

A complete reconstructed sheet of Great Britain, 1 penny black
In same order as on the original plate.

PLATING

The reconstruction of a sheet of stamps in the same original order as appeared on the printing plate. This is constructed by means of singles, pairs, strips and blocks. Practiced mostly on the earlier issues where crude or imperfect dies, plates or printing made possible many recognizable differences or inconsistencies among the individual stamps of a sheet. Plating requires patient and intensive research work which only a true philatelist will undertake.

PLEBISCITE ISSUES

Stamps issued in a territory during a period when a vote is being taken over its future sovereignty.

PONY EXPRESS

A mail service during pioneer days in the West just prior to the Civil War. Route was between St. Joseph, Mo., and San Francisco and other western points. Was discontinued after the extension of the telegraph to San Francisco as it could not withstand the competition. Adhesives of this legendary service are listed among locals in Scott's U. S. Specialized Catalog.

PORTE DE MAR STAMPS

Stamps utilized for the purpose of indicating the amount of postage to be prepaid to steamship companies for taking outbound mail.

POSTAL FISCALS (Postal Revenues)

The use of a postmark cancellation on fiscals (revenue stamps) in place of the regular revenue cancellation is generally accepted evidence that the stamp was used for mail matter against that for revenue purposes. Some foreign revenues (or fiscals) are overprinted "postal" for postal use.

PLAYING CARD STAMPS (U. S.)

Revenue stamps issued by the United States Government which are affixed by manufacturers on packs of playing cards to fulfill the payment of taxes.

POST OFFICE SEALS (U. S.)

Printed labels issued by the United States post office as mending paper to seal and repair mail matter which has been damaged or opened up in transit. Listed in Scott's United States Specialized Catalog.

POSTAL SAVINGS STAMPS (U. S.)

Not postage stamps but part of a plan to encourage accumulations of small amounts of 10c and up towards eventual conversion into U. S. Postal Savings Accounts. Listed in Scott's U.S. Specialized Catalog.

POSTMASTERS PROVISIONAL ISSUES

Issued by local postmasters of various towns before the regular United States government issues.

PREMIUM

From a stamp collector's viewpoint, this is a free offer or a low priced bargain offered in advertisements as an inducement to prospective applicants for selections of stamps on approval.

PRESIDENTIALS

Refers to the 1938-43 Presidential Stamp Series of U. S. Stamps, consisting of 32 varieties in which are included all presidents from George Washington to Calvin Coolidge in consecutive order of their terms in office. In addition there are also ½c Benjamin Franklin, 1½c Martha Washington and 4½c White House.

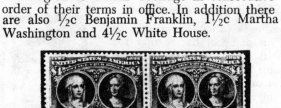

PRINTERS IMPRINT

Usually found on the margin of the sheet or underneath the stamp.

PRINTER'S WASTE

Philatelically this refers to faulty, incorrect or defective stampic or printed matter of the United States Printing Dept. which has been destroyed or destined to the trash basket. Although mostly valueless, rigid inspection is required to keep those potentially valuable pieces from leaking out.

PRO-DESOCUPADOS (OVERPRINTS)

Stamps so designated in Spanish by over-prints or so inscribed, etc. refers to unemployment fund issues.

PRO JUVENTUTE ISSUES

Semi Postal stamps of Switzerland issued annually since 1913. The surtax or amount in addition to postage is turned over to child welfare institutions.

PROPAGANDA WAR STAMPS

Refers particularly to imitations of German stamps by American and British governments. These symbolically played up Hitler and the Nazis as death, murderers, etc. Distributed by United States and British agents within enemy territory for the purpose of sowing discontent, undermining morale, and furthering defeatism.

PROPRIETARY STAMPS

For use in collecting revenue on various taxable commodities. Some of these stamps, were issued under government license from 1864 to 1900, were the famous Match and Medicine Stamps. Others have been issued by the government for general use.

QUARTZ LAMP

Largely used for the inspection and expertizing of stamps. Its ultra-violet rays are a great aid in analyzing the various substances of a stamp such as paper, ink, color, etc. Also will clearly reveal any doctoring or repairs of stamps as well as the removal of cancellations, penmarks, chemical cleaning and other changes the naked eye will not detect. Such instruments are available from Hanovia Chemical & Mfg. Co., Newark 5, N. J.

REDRAWN

This is when a design is redrawn and a new die is engraved in order to improve, change or correct any design already in use.

RE-ISSUE

A new printing of a discontinued issue. Often slight variations are to be found from the original printing.

RELIEF PRINTING

This applies to any process of printing whereby the surface stands up higher than that part of the plate which is not to be printed. The best example of this is Typography or Type Set printing.

REMAINDERS

Represents the unsold stock of stamps of a government issue after that particular issue has been succeeded by a new issue. These are often sold mint below face value or may be deliberately obliterated with either regular cancellation, bars, lines, etc. so that they cannot be used for postal duty. When sold the issue is usually demonetized so that they will be no longer valid for postage.

The first stamp is from flat plate. The other from Rotary plate.

ROTARY PRESS PRINTING

Stamps printed on a rotary press. Its plates are curved so as to revolve around a cylinder. The paper is continuously fed from a long roll. Rotary Press stamps are usually slightly longer or wider than those of the flat press. This is due to the extra space needed for the curvature of the cylinder plate.

ROOSEVELTS

These refer to the stamps or sets issued by various countries throughout the world in honor of President Franklin D. Roosevelt, after his death on April 12, 1945.

SECRET MARKS

Made by an engraver of a die to distinguish his work. Of special interest, reference is made to the United States issue of 1873. See Continental Bank Note Co.

SERIFS

Small strokes or lines added to the plain ends of letters to afford some ornamention.

SANS SERIF (WITHOUT SERIFS)

Refers to a style of lettering on stamps in which the ends of such are plain and not fancy or ornamental. For example, see Norway 1926-34 Issues.

SET OF STAMPS

A specific complete or incomplete issue of stamps. May consist of only one stamp as long as it constitutes a complete issue. Otherwise it would come under the status of a single stamp. Sets are described as complete when they contain all the stamps of the entire series. It is considered a short set when it consists of only part of the series but no less than two stamps.

SILVER JUBILEE ISSUES

A series of issues used throughout the British Empire in 1935 in commemoration of the 25th Anniversary of the rule of King George V.

SLEEPER

This is descriptive of an exceptional stamp that has been acquired at a low price due to having been overlooked or passed up as a much cheaper stamp.

SLURRED IMPRESSIONS

As distinguished from double print. This is usually due to shift of paper during printing.

SPACE FILLER

This is a stamp not up to desired standards in condition but nevertheless occupying the correct space awaiting a better copy. Among discriminating collectors, stamps with straight edges, heavy cancellations, thin spots, or any kind of fault or defect would be utilized only as space fillers.

SPECIALIST

A devotee of stamp collecting whose ardor goes beyond the mere accumulation of stamps. Will engage in philatelic study, research and endeavor. This may extend to the inclusion of related but non-philatelic, illustrative, historical, and descriptive matter.

SPECIALIZED COLLECTION

Limited to a group, country or to only one stamp. The details and variations may cover a wide range of minor varieties, depending upon the research and zeal of the collector.

SAMPLE

Overprinted on a stamp. Submitted by a government to contractors for estimates on the printing of said specimen.

SPECIAL PRINTINGS

An example of this is the re-issuance of the National Parks and other U. S. Commemoratives in complete inperforate sheets for sale to the public. This was to satisfy protests by collectors against the post office originally printing a limited quantity in favor of certain government and political figures. Generally, the term Special Printing is interpreted to mean current stamps being issued in special form of miniature sheets for philatelic exhibitions, public celebrations, etc.

SPECIMEN

Philatelically this has two interpretations. First, specimen may simply mean a stamp. Secondly, specimen printed across a stamp serves as a cancellation to prevent its future use. This is when first copies of new stamps are submitted to the Universal Postal Union to be distributed as samples to its member countries. This practice is now seldom observed.

STONE PRINTING

By use of stone plates. Details not as sharp or as bright as engravings from metal plates. The difference is easily noticeable in comparative cases.

STAGE COACH MAIL

Was in extensive use until the railroad reduced and finally eliminated this former romantic service. Adhesives of private companies like Wells Fargo & Co operated these routes and are listed in Scott's U. S. Specialized Catalog.

STOCK TRANSFER U. S. REVENUE STAMPS

For use in the collection of a tax on all transactions involving the sale, delivery or transfers of shares of stock.

SUEZ CANAL STAMPS (PRIVATE ISSUE)

Issued by the Suez Canal Company in July 1868 for posts along the canal route. Four varieties were issued although only the 20c denomination was authorized. However, a few of the other three varieties, 1c, 5c and 40c, are known to have been used. The service was suspended in August 1868 and the remaining stamps sold to dealers. Many counterfeits are known to have been made of this issue.

SUNDAY DELIVERY STAMPS

Good examples of such special Sunday delivery stamps are Bulgaria 1925-41 Postal Tax Issues. These stamps were attached if delivery of the letters was necessary on Sundays or holidays.

SUNDAY (DOMINICAL LABELS) ISSUES

These are the small tabs or labels usually attached to such stamps as Belgium 1893-1914 issues. Thereon are printed instructions not to deliver on Sunday. If delivery on Sunday is desired, the label had to be detached.

60g is the normal postage. The 20g additional is the surtax.

SURTAX

Usually on charity or semi-postal issues. In addition to amount of postage there is included an extra amount (or surtax) for the benefit of some specific charity or purpose.

TABS

Attached to or part of a stamp. May be in nature of advertisement, propaganda, public interest or information relating to illustration or stamps.

TELEGRAPH STAMPS

Issued by private companies in connection with telegraph charges. Those of the United States are listed in Scott's United States Specialized Catalog.

TELEGRAPH POSTALS

Although these are usually of private issue with prepayment of charges, some of them have been used for postal duty. If authentic they are known as Postal Telegraph Stamps.

THEMATICS (see TOPICALS)

TIED ON

This is where the impression of an original postmark or cancellation reaches beyond the stamp to the cover or attached paper. This tie up is accepted as substantiating proof of such a condition. May apply to covers, bisects, and other pieces where the "tie on" factor is significant.

TIMBRE

A common term especially on stamps of France and French Colonies. The meaning is "postage stamps."

TOBACCO SALES TAX STAMPS

Applying to United States. To facilitate the collection of revenue on general sales of tobacco. Listed in Scott's United States Specialized Catalog.

TOO LATE ISSUES

These refer to stamps planned for postal duty, but upon completion of printing it was never possible to put the stamps into use on account of enemy occupancy, insurrection, etc.

TOPICALS (Thematics)

This refers to stamps classified according to a certain subject or that illustrated in its design. As examples topicals may comprise groups such as Animals, Fish, Statues, Butterflies, etc.

STAMPS AS A SOUND INVESTMENT

As indisputable testimony to the increasing soundness and respect that philatelic values have impressed upon both connoisseurs and investors alike, there have been many amazing world records broken price-wise. Among these was the legendary British Guiana 1956 1¢ magenta which reached the all time high for a single stamp when sold at the Siegel Auction Galleries on April 24, 1970 for $280,000. This formerly sold in 1940 for $45,000. Another world record was broken at the H. R. Harmer auction on Oct. 21, 1968. This was for a 1847 Mauritius cover with two superlative copies of the 1¢ penny orange which sold for the all time world record high price of $380,000 for a philatelic item. It came from the collection of the late Mrs. Louise Boyd Dale. Formerly purchased for $250. At the Robson Lowe sale in London on March 26, 1970, a rare British Guiana 1951 cover with a pair of circular "Cotton Reels" was sold for the unprecedented high price of £75,000. (or $180,000). Another new top price of $34,000. was paid by Irwin Weinberg for a copy of the 24¢ U.S. bi-colored invert. Also at the same sale there was purchased by him for $32,000. a copy of the 1869 U.S. 30¢ with flags inverted. These represent a big breakthrough in philatelic values with greatly enhanced prestige for the hobby.

TYPE SET

Refers to stamps printed from printer's type and not from an engraved die or plate.

TYPEWRITTEN STAMPS

Stamps issued by means of a typewriter. For examples of these see Uganda 1895-6 Issues. The latter stamps were produced with a typewriter by the Rev. E. Miller of the Church Missionary Society. Listed in Scott's No. 1 to 53.

Some Universal Postal Union (U.P.U.) Commemoratives.

UNIVERSAL POSTAL UNION (U. P. U.)

An organization started in 1875 to regulate the interchange of mail matter among member countries. Since then almost every country in the world has joined.

UNLISTED STAMPS

This ordinarily implies that the stamp in question has been denied a listing in a standard catalog as for instance in Scott's. Among various reasons for the unacceptability may be that the stamps are of a non-existent government, of bogus origin, of private nature, issued for sale for sole purpose of sale to stamp collectors without intent to serve postal duty. Sometimes, a stamp may receive belated recognition or be dropped after being listed for many years. Also less important stamps or issues have been dropped from listing as an economy move to save space in catalog. Time may be lost in trying to locate in the catalog the listing of foreign revenues which look similar to stamps. These are not listed in Scott's unless postally used. Foreign envelope stamps, postal cards and telegraph stamps are likewise not listed in Scott's Standard Catalog.

VALUE OF STAMPS

The most convenient method is to look these up in a standard catalog but such values should be accepted only tentatively. Another basis is the face value of a specimen. The value may be altered one way or the other depending upon the fluctuations in the market as well as in currency rates. Auctions are another basis. This may be influenced however by conditions or circumstances. However the law of supply and demand is always a very reliable barometer and this can be best availed of by studiously watching the market through advertisements, price lists, philatelic literature, etc.

VARIETY

A difference in a stamp which distinguishes it from any other. This may be very obvious, of slightest degree, or even unnoticeable as in the case of watermarks.

VIGNETTE

The central illustration or design of a stamp. May be portrait, scene, structure, symbol, etc. This is aside from the framework including inscriptions.

WANT LIST

This represents a list of stamps especially sought after by a collector. It is logical to presume that in this list would be included specimens particularly needed to complete sets, countries, etc., and those difficult to find in the past. In making up this list it would be helpful to mention whether mint or used specimens are required. Also mention catalog number, condition and top paying price. As a want list usually requires considerable search, time and effort, it should not be given to more than one dealer at a time. It would be mutually beneficial to both parties if a definite time limit is given. To the buyer it restores freedom of action if necessary to look elsewhere and he will not be faced in the future with a purchase no longer needed. To the dealer the customer is under an implied obligation during the specified time limit for the wanted stamps.

WAR (or Defense) SAVINGS STAMPS

Part of a governmental savings plan to encourage the savings of small amounts from 10c and up for eventual conversion into U. S. Treasury Certificates, War or Defense Bonds.

WESTERN FRANKS (U. S.)

Refers to express companies such as Wells, Fargo Co., and the Pony Express, which undertook early mail service to points beyond regular government delivery, especially over wild and hazardous Western routes. These independent companies usually utilized the regular government stamped envelopes over which were printed their own private franks.

WIRE CLOTH

The wire cloth stretched across the mould in the manufacture of paper which determines the texture of the material. Also the watermark design is attached to this wire cloth.

WOOD BLOCKS

Blocks of wood into which the design was cut. Utilized only among the early issues.

ZEPS

The nickname for the special set of Graf Zeppelin stamps issued by the U. S. in 1930.

ZIP CODE

Represents a system to speed up U.S. mail by means of a five number numeral. By using this numeral as part of the address, post office clerks can ascertain the part of the country, state and post office to which mail matter is destined.

10003

ZIP BLOCK

A block of United States stamps bearing that margin of the sheet or pane on which appears the sketch "Mr. Zip." The first of these was the Sam Houston Commemorative.

USE ZIP CODE

184

185

ERNEST A. KEHR
Stamp Editor:
Active in
"Stamps for wounded."
New York, N. Y.

PETER G. KELLER
1894-1972
Former famous
A.S.D.A. executive

KURT WEISHAUPT
Former President
American Stamp
Dealers Association